Ferrari

Ferrari

Rainer W. Schlegelmilch
Hartmut Lehbrink
Jochen von Osterroth

KÖNEMANN

Contents

250 GT 40

375 Plus 44

750 Monza 48

410 S 52

335 S 84

250 GT Cabriolet PF 90

250 GT California Spyder SWB 94

250 GT Coupé PF 102

250 GTO 132

250 GT Lusso 142

250 LM 148

330 GT 2+2 154

365 California 192

Dino 206 S 198

712 CanAm 204

365 GT 2+2 210

312 PB 236

365 GTC/4 240

BB 512i 244

412 252

F512 M 282

F40 290

348 ts 300

456 GT 308

360 Spider 338

Enzo Ferrari 350

Challenge Stradale 360

612 Scaglietti 370

Preface

Ferrari and motor racing are two sides of the same coin, deeply etched into the very nature of the man Enzo Ferrari. He lived to win whatever the stakes, whether as a driver, a team manager or a constructor. It is but a short step from a Ferrari Grand Prix car, the most radical expression of the car maker's art, to a Grand Tourer of the same marque.

It is obvious to the ear, because a Ferrari, any Ferrari, even one built to comply with the most stringent and mundane emission control regulations, still has a whisper of the legend of Le Mans, Monza and the Targa Florio. It is a legend based on a fifty-year history in motor sport.

It is equally obvious to the eye. Designed by artists like Michelotti or Pininfarina, the prototypes, the sports cars and the road-going coupés that bear the black prancing horse coat of arms have a unique style that speeds them on their way from the start to the chequered flag or from Paris to Rome in the blink of an eye.

These famous lines have evolved out of the search for performance and this book traces that story in words and images. While covering the cars, the engines and the men who made them, it also underlines the fact that competition is the mother of invention.

This is an on-going story that does not necessarily reach a climax at its conclusion. At the beginning, just as at the end, we find a Barchetta. The path that links them is strewn with the most powerful images of pure beauty and charisma that can be conjured up in the name of the motor car.

Given the abundance of creativity that marked the beginning of our story in particular, the authors have not attempted to portray the complete picture, but have contented themselves with producing an outline sketch. This has sometimes led to a subjective view of the story.

Preface by Luca Cordero di Montezemolo

Every time a new book appears about Ferrari, I ask myself why a subject that has been covered so often can still be so interesting. As for this book, it has impressed me above all with the quality of the text, the accuracy of the information and the clarity of the illustrations.

When I am asked what I think of the cars designed and built by Ferrari, I reply that I have always liked and admired them. That is to say, a long time before I became the Scuderia's Sporting Director, and then, twenty years later, the President of the company.

I too have fallen under the spell that emanates from every creation bearing the sign of the *cavallino rampante*, and I have often asked myself why. Now that I am directly involved with this phenomenon and can see it from the inside, I think I have found the answer.

Ferraris have been described in a thousand and one ways, and the imagination of the writers who have tackled the subject has already used up all the superlatives.

"The epitome of mechanical beauty acquired by men who want to turn their dreams into reality and inject their life with a long period of youthful passion" was a favourite expression of our founder, Enzo Ferrari. With time, other concepts were added to this romantic image, such as the advance of civilization, culture and the arts.

This high regard presents us with a great challenge in our work, because we have to prove ourselves worthy of it so that what might be called the "Ferrari effect" will never lose its spell. It is precisely this sentimental aspect which reinforces a deeply held personal conviction: Ferrari today embodies the logical evolution of a tradition based on its fifty-year history. The secret of success is to continue to develop and to put forward objects that bear the stamp of emotion.

Luca Cordero di Montezemolo
President of Ferrari

Ferrari

The Man

More than any others, three men have made a lasting impression on a century of the motor car: Henry Ford provided the prose, in that he produced transport for the masses; Ettore Bugatti and Enzo Ferrari on the other hand provided the poetry, deliberately dedicating themselves to realising our dreams. These two men were only rivals in the timeless world of legend, the Italian colossus beginning his work at the end of the 1940s when the French giant of Italian descent was coming to the end of his career.

Enzo Ferrari was a man of the world in as much as the world came knocking on his door, while his reputation spread far and wide. However he was very much a local boy. He was born on 18th February 1898 in Modena, into a reasonably well-off family, and for most of his life he stayed within the magical triangle of Modena, Maranello and Fiorano; a sort of secular Vatican, and indeed it was in Modena that he died on 14th August 1988.

"I am coming up to the finishing line", he said in 1987 as he celebrated his company's fortieth birthday. Even though they could see the sense in his remark, it was an emotional moment for his audience. The aristocratic Count Giovanni Lurani Cernuschi, a racer and journalist who had been Ferrari's friend for sixty years, put this remark into perspective, writing after his death: "Ferrari was always in pole position, whether as a driver, a team owner, a constructor of racing and prestigious cars, or a motivator of men and ideas."

Enzo Ferrari's career as a driver was played out in two distinct halves, separated by a two year gap when he sharpened his talent and polished his act. He made a modest debut on 5th October 1919, finishing fifth in class and twelfth overall at the Parma–Poggio di Berceto hillclimb. He was at the wheel of a CMN (Costruzioni Meccaniche Nazionali) made from a collection of Isotta-Fraschini parts. The high point of this part of his career came in 1920 when he finished second in the Targa Florio. By that time Ferrari was already an official Alfa Romeo driver and he could have actually won the race if he had been better informed by his team as to what was going on in the hills and valleys of Madonia. The curtain came down on this part of his life in mysterious circumstances during the 1924 Grand Prix of Europe at Lyon. In practice, he completed a few laps then left the circuit and returned to Modena by train. No explanation was ever forthcoming.

The second half kicked off with a bang in 1927, with wins in Alessandria and Modena. Unfortunately this early promise was not fulfilled and the final act was played out in 1931 on the Three Provinces track. In what was to prove a symbolic humiliation, Ferrari was beaten by a whisker by Tazio Nuvolari. In other words the boss had had to give way to the employee. On 1st December 1929, in the presence of the well-known man of law, Enzo Levi, the Società Anonima Scuderia Ferrari, (the Ferrari Team) had been founded. This organization was tasked to run a motor sport programme on behalf of Alfa Romeo, under the leadership of Enzo Ferrari. Committed to succeed, Ferrari decided to hire the best possible drivers. One of them was Tazio Nuvolari, then embarking on what would

At the wheel: Alfa-Romeo's works driver Enzo Ferrari at the beginning of his career in 1920, with his wife beside him and surrounded by his colleagues Baconin Borzacchini, Luigi Arcangeli and Tazio Nuvolari.

Alfa pilots Tazio Nuvolari and Baconin Borzacchini – the Scuderia Ferrari logo can be seen on the side of the vehicle.

be a glorious career. Despite great wins in the 1932 Targa Florio, the 1933 Mille Miglia, and the 1935 German Grand Prix at the Nürburgring, where Nuvolari beat a whole host of Silver Arrows, conflict was always on the cards between Enzo Ferrari and Tazio Nuvolari. This conflict was to set the tone for the *Ingegnere*'s future relationships with his drivers.

1935 signalled the first brief appearances of his own cars: two twin-engined single-seaters with front and rear-mounted eight cylinder Alfa Romeo engines, even though the Portello based marque adopted them as their own. These cars were extremely reliable and capable of over 300 km (185 miles) per hour, but were handicapped by excessive tyre wear.

On 1st January 1938 Alfa Romeo announced its intention to run its own race team under the Alfa Corse banner. At the same time Enzo Ferrari was offered the position of Sporting Director in this new organisation. His signature on the contract was a time bomb which in 1939 led to him leaving the company with some of his closest colleagues like Luigi Bazzi and Alberto Massimino. The reason for this divorce, Italian style, was the constant tension existing between Ferrari and Alfa Romeo director, Ugo Gobbato. But the final detonator for his departure was Ferrari's lack of respect for Ricart, the Spanish engineer. Ferrari did not hide his disdain for the Spaniard, going so far as to accuse him of having lank oily hair and of shirking his responsibilities. He went further, saying that shaking hands with the Spaniard was like holding a soft piece of boneless meat, as lifeless as a corpse.

When it came to appearances Ferrari was always an aesthete. He would make a caustic study of his entourage, taking persistent delight in revealing unsavoury details about people. He had this to say, with a note of disgust in his voice, when describing Giuseppe Campari, a star driver for the Scuderia, with whom he enjoyed a cordial and friendly relationship. "His body was covered with black down which hid his pinkish skin, almost always shining with beads of perspiration."

But in the case of his split with Alfa Romeo, the reasons for the disagreement went much deeper: Ferrari was no longer disposed to be a subordinate. Furthermore he felt that if one stayed too long working for the same company, one lost the sense of initiative. Finally he had legitimate reasons for seeking revenge.

The directors of Alfa Romeo had forbidden him to build or to race any car at all under his own name for a period of four years. Despite this, back in Modena, Enzo Ferrari formed a company under the anodyne name of "Auto Avio Costruzioni" and built two very handsome spider-type 815s with bodywork by Touring, to compete in the 1940 Mille Miglia. For all that, these cars bore an uncanny resemblance to the

1929 – Enzo Ferrari's first independent step: he sets up Scuderia Ferrari – Alfa's racing sport department as an outsourcing model, as it were.

Enzo Ferrari with the Scuderia pilots Antonio Brivio, Carlo Felice Trossi and Tazio Nuvolari in Alessandria in 1933.

A great year for Ferrari, in 1951 José Froilán Gonzalez (here at the GP in Germany) wins against Alfa.

Alfa Romeo 2300 6C. On 14th July 1951, when Froilán Gonzalez – "The Pampas Bull" – won the British Grand Prix at the wheel of a Ferrari 375 F1 defeating the previously invincible Alfetta 159s, Enzo Ferrari had no hesitation in announcing: "I have killed my own mother!"

The first twelve cylinder engine to carry his name appeared in 1946 and was the brainchild of engine specialist Gioachino Colombo and engineer Luigi Bazzi. The power unit had a capacity of one and half litres; each cylinder displacing 125 cc. This produced its model name: the 125. Cylinders by the dozen were not common currency in the post-war years, but Ferrari was something of a visionary and was prepared

The power and luck of his emblem was to be passed on to Enzo Ferrari: fighter pilot Francesco Baracca, whose biplane was adorned with a black horse – il cavallino rampante – on a yellow background.

to bet on the future. He had admired the qualities of the twelve cylinder engines produced by Delage and Packard and had fallen in love with this sophisticated piece of machinery and with what he described, in true Italian style, as the "song of the twelve". Thus the way was paved for a lifelong fascination.

Nothing seemed to rattle Enzo Ferrari. On 18th June 1969 Giovanni Agnelli, the powerful boss of the Fiat group, acquired half the shares of the Ferrari company, but the man himself, now relegated to the role of controller of an empire that had once been his own, was still as vigorous, vital and brilliant as ever. His annual press conference remained, as ever, a meeting with a monument; a private meeting, the equivalent of a papal audience. He was a Renaissance prince of the twentieth century with a grasp of the teachings of Machiavelli. He could keep royalty, celebrities and the monied classes at bay by following to the letter the simple expedient of keeping them waiting.

For those who depended on him but had the misfortune to fall from grace, particularly drivers who no

The Commendatore never got over his death: his son Alfredo "Dino" Ferrari, who died young of leukaemia in 1956.

longer contributed or appeared not to contribute to the grand reputation of his company, he reserved a whole host of atrocities, from the simple scalpel cut to the scaffold. Past achievements counted for nothing. Motor racing masters like John Surtees and Jacky Ickx have both felt his anger. Incurring the wrath of a man of Enzo Ferrari's stature was to experience a reign of terror, as he knew how to pull strings in his favour, knowing that no one likes to cross a monument.

His own experience had taught Ferrari how to manipulate reality, and he worked on and polished this image with well thought-out brush strokes. A case in point is the uncertain origin of the little black horse emblem prancing on the yellow background of the town of Modena. He himself came up with the following explanation: on 25th May 1923, after winning at the Savio track near Ravenna, he was sought out by the parents of war hero Francesco Baracca. Baracca was a legendary airman who had shot down 34 enemy aircraft before being shot down himself in the hills of Montello shortly before the end of the war. His emblem was a prancing horse and according to Ferrari, the countess Paolina Baracca presented him with this heraldic device on the spur of the moment, saying, "Ferrari, take this. Put it on your cars and it will bring you luck."

Some people claim that this chivalrous gesture exceeded the countess' competence; that the little horse was simply the emblem of the squadron and was still being used as a coat of arms by an *aerobrigata* after the Second World War.

There is yet another dubious legend in the myth that is Ferrari. The story goes that, while competing in his first Targa Florio in 1919, his CMN got stuck in the procession of cars following the Italian President, Vittorio Orlando, on his way to make a speech in Campofelice. The record shows that Orlando was definitely in Sicily that day, but in Termini Imerese, a particularly popular resort with Targa Florio competitors.

Finally, there is a third anecdote that would seem to be quite simply the result of an overactive imagination. During one particular race we are to believe that Ferrari got caught in a snow storm and was attacked by wolves. A situation that is hard to imagine, even for the most ardent fan of winter rallying!

It is impossible to describe Ferrari's character in conventional terms. Not that it was uncertain or lacked glamour. The biggest problem is that he was an extremely diverse character and impossible to categorize. While the made-to-measure cliché of a realist fits Ferrari perfectly, he nevertheless had a fatalist streak, and like many creative people he suffered from a degree of melancholia. "I feel lost and subject to the whim of destiny", he would sometimes complain with typical Latin self-pity.

He seemed to have an almost intimate relationship with death and knew it by sight as it were, "a nodding acquaintance with death", as Stirling Moss put it.

Enzo Ferrari never got over the death of his son, who died of leukaemia in 1956, and in his honour several engines and cars bore the shortened version of his name – Dino. The list of drivers who died carrying the Ferrari emblem reads like a huge posthumous race grid, Giuseppe Campari, Alberto Ascari, Eugenio Castellotti, Luigi Musso, Peter Collins, Ken Wharton, Alfonso de Portago, Wolfgang von Trips, Tommy Spychiger, Lorenzo Bandini and Gilles Villeneuve to name but a few.

Just like Joe Keller in Arthur Miller's *All My Sons,* who is ridden by pangs of remorse because of the pilots that have died through his fault, so too Enzo Ferrari suffered terribly. But in fact, most accidents to Ferrari drivers were caused by human error. Each time he would react to the standard barrage from the media by hiding ever more deeply in his Modena hermitage, where he could go to find himself. Apart from a few lightning visits to Monza, he hardly ever came to the track. Not because he disliked travel, but because, in his mind, his cars were living things, and also because he either loved or hated his drivers. When he loved them he was forgiving, which is why he called the daredevil Gilles Villeneuve his Prince of Destruction.

His self-imposed solitude had a double effect. On the one hand the old man's view of the world came to him filtered and described by his colleagues in a way that suited him, while on the other hand the outside world would only hear what he felt they wanted to hear. John Surtees, who was World Champion with Ferrari in 1964, compared Maranello in the sixties to a castle surrounded by a moat with only a drawbridge for access.

This led to a constant conflict with the press who were ceaselessly searching for information. But at least opinions on the iron-willed autocrat were divided. Franco Lini, a journalist who was also Ferrari's Sporting Director for two years from 1966, claims that Ferrari would devote a lot of time to studying people to see if they could be useful to him, and to study their strengths and weaknesses, as if he X-rayed them.

He would remain loyal to faithful colleagues, or at least for as long as they were in his service.

With his usual frankness and no beating about the bush, Niki Lauda, World Champion at the wheel of a Ferrari in 1975 and 1977, declares: "Enzo Ferrari? An ancient statue with a will of iron. You had to take him at face value, either that or you would last no longer than a month in his company."

As for Giancarlo Baghetti, now a director of *Auto Oggi* in Milan, he learnt all there was to learn about the sphinx that was Ferrari. "Our first meeting took

place in January 1961. His welcome was as icy as the weather that day. But I suppose I made a good impression as he took me into the team."

Baghetti rewarded him for this in a way that remains unique in the statistic books. He won the French Grand Prix at Reims that year, his maiden Grand Prix. After a while their relationship cooled as Baghetti left the Scuderia of his own accord. "I saw him again for the first time at Monza, during practice for the 1966 Italian Grand Prix. It was the first year of the three litre Formula One cars. I felt ill at ease, a bit like a deserter. But Ferrari was cheerful and pleasant with me." During first practice, Baghetti, at the wheel of a Lotus-BRM, had not done particularly well, and Ferrari came to talk to him. "There is still one Dino 246 at Maranello. Would you like to drive it?" Silent with emotion, Baghetti could only agree.

The next day the car was at his disposal.

John Surtees, pictured here at the German Grand Prix at the Nürburg-ring, experienced as a Ferrari pilot from 1963 to 1966 the various facets of his employer's personality.

Giancarlo Baghetti, the later winner of the Grand Prix de France 1961, with colleagues Willy Mairesse and Lorenzo Bandini behind a Dino 156 F1.

Ferrari

The Marque

In the beginning there was an engine, a twelve cylinder. It was 1946, and in its own way this engine epitomised the rebirth of Italy after the war. But it was also a symbol of Enzo Ferrari's single-minded will to follow his chosen path, with no consideration for any obstacles put in his way. It would not take long for events to prove him right, events in the shape of his success in competition and the fact that he spawned imitators more or less all over the place – surely the sincerest form of flattery. Right from the beginning, Ferrari, as a constructor, made the engine his priority with the chassis coming second. For the bodywork he looked elsewhere. As Battista Farina, who was Ferrari's favourite coachbuilder from 1952, liked to say, "one of us was looking for a beautiful and famous lady to dress, and the other was trying to find a tailor who would produce made-to-measure garments for her".

The sectional drawing of Ferrari opus 1, published in the Italian press in the winter of 1946/47, proved this concept: while every precise detail of the engine, the frame and suspension was clearly visible, the silhouette of a coupé was vague and sketchy. In fact the first car to come out of the Maranello factory carrying the prancing horse badge was a spider which predicted the lines of future "barchettas".

The 125 Sport was a Ferrari-red challenge. His aim was obvious. He had to beat the enemy, Alfa Romeo, where it would hurt the most, in other words in Formula 1. Enzo Ferrari planned the campaign down to the last detail, refining his strategy and involving himself in every aspect of the task in a variety of classes including Sports Cars, Grand Touring cars, Formula 2 and Formula Libre.

At the same time he strengthened his position with the solid support of engineers like Gioachino Colombo, who had been with him in the early days and would stay with Ferrari until 1951, and Aurelio Lampredi who never deserted his post from 1948 to 1955. They were the creators of the 125 and 159 models and later of the 166, 195, 212, 225, 275, 340 and 375. These numbers denoting the different versions simply indicated the capacity of a single cylinder. One only has to perform the simple task of multiplying them by the magic number 12 to find the cubic capacity of the engine. By 1950 the maximum capacity allowed for a normally aspirated engine of 4.5 litres was reached and this rule would apply until the end of the following year. The Alfetta 158 and 159 ran with 1.5 supercharged engines under the equivalence rule. The irony of this was that Ferrari was now battling with his own past, as this concept, dating back to the thirties, had been created by himself, Gioachino Colombo and Luigi Bazzi.

In 1950, the first season of the modern era of Grand Prix racing, the battle ended in a humiliating five-nil defeat. But in the course of the following season,

The Ferrari Lancia of the year 1956 – Luigi Musso at the wheel. The aerodynamically advantageous fairings between the front and the rear tires were a peculiarity of this vehicle, which was originally designed for Lancia.

Battista "Pinin" Farina – the great little coachbuilder, whose cooperation with Enzo Ferrari outlasted the death of both men, and still continues today. The photograph shows both men in Modena in 1963.

during which Ferrari triumphed at Silverstone with Froilán Gonzalez and with Alberto Ascari at both Nürburgring and Monza, the great leap towards immortality had been made.

By now the Ferrari name – very common in Italy but enjoying cult status when applied to a motor car – had a good ring to it in competition circles.

On 25th May 1947, 44-year-old Franco Cortese had won the 125 Sport's second ever race on the Caracalla circuit in Rome.

The first international win for a Ferrari followed on 11th October of the same year at Turin, with Raymond "Lionheart" Sommer at the wheel of a two-seater 159 S. When Froilán Gonzalez won the British Grand Prix on 14th July 1951, the victory could be seen as a fitting epilogue to innumerable victories in sports car events: the 1949 Targa Florio with Biondetti/Benedetti; 1949 Mille Miglia, with Biondetti/Salani and the Mille Miglia yet again in 1950 with Giannino Marzotto (one of three racing heirs to a textiles empire) partnered by Marco Crosara; and still the Mille Miglia the next year with Villoresi/Cassani; as well as Le Mans in 1949 with the Luigi Chinetti/Lord Selsdon pairing.

By 1950 Enzo Ferrari already employed 200 people, but he was still not a rich man, as he depended to a large extent on fees and prize money from his wins. Even such famous factory drivers as Tazio Nuvolari, Alberto Ascari and Felice Bonetto had to hand over fifty percent of their winnings, which in fact only barely covered expenses.

So Ferrari decided to add a second string to his bow to fill his coffers, namely the production of high speed road cars which, to this day, continue to support the company's racing activities. At a press conference in February 1995 to launch the 412 T2 single-seater for that season's racing, Ferrari President Luca di Montezemolo explained that fifty-five percent of the competition budget came from sponsors and the factory had to find the rest.

For the first four years it was hard to spot the difference between the racing cars and the grand touring cars, except that the latters' chassis were always given odd numbers. To prove the point, Gianni Marzotto twice ran in the Mille Miglia in cars which he used on a daily basis to drive to work.

At first Enzo Ferrari looked after his customers personally, but he soon put a network into place with major local dealers like Luigi Chinetti in New York and Colonel Ronnie Hoare of Maranello Concessionaires in London. Sales brochures were rare and unnecessary as the cars were much loved thanks to their reputation in competition. Effectively this thoroughbred product from the Emilia Romana region with its bodywork produced by such metalwork masters as Vignale, Ghia, Touring and the master

A change of drivers in 1953: the two Ferrari pilots Luigi "Gigi" Villoresi and Alberto Ascari at the German Grand Prix at the Nürburgring

builder Stabilimenti Farina was its own best advertisement for power, fame and beauty. Each Ferrari was made to measure and virtually unique.

In 1951 in a Tortona restaurant a crucial meeting took place between Enzo Ferrari, Battista "Pinin" Farina and his son Sergio. The planning of this meeting led to some argument. Ferrari did not want to leave Maranello and Farina wanted to stay in his kingdom of Turin. Finally they met on neutral ground. The two men knew one another since the Aosta–Grand St. Bernard hillclimb in 1921 and they had followed one another's fortunes ever since, although neither would admit as much. The prophets of doom had predicted that a meeting of these two strong personalities would be akin to putting two operatic prima donnas on the same billing. As things turned out it would lead to a lifelong dialogue. "We go together as well as the colours of blue and yellow", Farina would later write.

Known in Italy as the "Consular Treaty", the fruits of this meeting were not long in coming, in the shape of a simple cabriolet destined for the Genevan team owner, Georges Filipinetti, followed by other one-offs and cars produced in small numbers such as the 375 America and the 250 GT Europa which were sold to a wealthy clientele. It was not until 1960 and the launch

The great Juan Manuel Fangio at the pit stop in Syracuse in 1956. This Grand Prix did not count towards the championship; Fangio won the race in this year for the fourth time, in a Ferrari Lancia D 50 – an eight-cylinder with 256 bhp.

of the 250 GTE 2+2, of which 955 were built, that one could really talk in terms of a production car.

That year there was one other important sign that Ferrari had decided to move with the times. Until then, the company revolved around the man, but now it was transformed into a limited company – Società Esercizio Fabbriche Automobili e Corse, or SEFAC.

Enzo Ferrari reckoned he had three distinctly different types of customer; the fifty-year-old who had done well in life; the motor sport enthusiast who felt he was an exceptional driver; and the playboy whose seductive girlfriend would bring everything to a standstill when she visited the workshop. But difficult times loomed on the horizon. SEFAC had diversified into Formula 1, Sports Prototypes and GT racing. Frequent changes to the technical regulations introduced by the CSI, the Paris-based sporting authority of the day, caused considerable expense for the constructors. There was also a growth of strong competition in the high performance road car market from companies like Porsche, Maserati, Jaguar and others such as Aston Martin.

It was at this point that one of the giants of the motor industry offered Ferrari its support. Henry Ford II, who was known to drive a black Ferrari when off-duty, approached the Commendatore. But the agreement which should have been signed on 20th May 1963 never saw the light of day as the Dearborn deity refused to allow Ferrari a free hand when it came to his pet project – the competition department.

Henry Ford did not take kindly to being snubbed in this way and swore he would get his revenge on Ferrari's favourite battleground. In 1964 a Daytona coupé prepared by one of Ford's partners, Carroll Shelby, won the GT category at Le Mans. Two years later, Chris Amon partnered by Bruce McLaren took overall victory in this legendary event at the wheel of a powerful Ford, powered by an impressive seven litre

V8. A Ford four-year hegemony at the Le Mans 24 Hours had thus begun. This did not stop the Ferrari 275 P and the 330 P (later the P2, P3 and P4) from winning several other endurance races.

This was not enough to calm the turbulent financial waters, however, and Ferrari was forced to humbly follow the road to Canossa, in this case to Turin, and to be precise to the Fiat headquarters. On 18th June 1969, the king of Maranello sold fifty percent of the shares in SEFAC to Gianni Agnelli, who was at all times polite and showed no sign of gloating over his acquisition. The agreement stated that on Ferrari's death, forty percent of the shares would revert to the Fiat group and ten percent would remain the property of his son, Piero Lardi Ferrari.

Thus it was that Enzo Ferrari, suitably reassured about the long-term future of his company, left the eighth floor office of the Fiat building at 10 Corso Marconi. Not only was the future of his business guaranteed, but also his position on the board was safe, irrespective of his age, and furthermore he retained personal control of the competition department.

Unwittingly the CSI had contributed to this partnership. In January 1965, two representatives from Fiat had visited Maranello with the aim of acquiring an engine to power two high performance models, a coupé and a cabriolet. It so happened that they arrived just as a compact two litre V6 engine designed by Franco Rocchi was being bench tested. An agreement was quickly reached and Fiat agreed to produce 500 cars by the end of the year. This was exactly the minimum number stipulated in the regulations, so that a version of this engine could be used in Formula 2 from the beginning of 1967.

The 365 GTB/4 was to be the first Ferrari to see the light of day under the patronage of Fiat, the last front-engined two seater high performance coupé. The Daytona, as it was called, was a phenomenal success and no less than 1395 were built between 1968 and 1973.

Then, despite a well planned product range, from the 308 GT4 to the BB 512, the successful sales story faltered slightly. Petrol crises, trouble with the trade unions, terrorist attacks organised by the Red Brigades, these were all factors which combined to create a general lack of confidence. There was still one ray of hope in the recessionary times of the mid-seventies, however, and that was the dominance of the Ferrari 312 T in Formula 1 against opponents generally using Ford engines.

The momentum that followed this period was characterised by almost constant progress. Cars such as the Ferrari 288 GTO and the F40, introduced to commemorate the fortieth anniversary of the company's existence, passed straight into motoring history, confirming the worth of both the man and his work. While some thought the death of Enzo Ferrari in August 1988 would diminish the value of his creations, they were wrong. In fact quite the opposite was true. Thanks to diehard speculators, the price of anything bearing the Ferrari emblem went through the roof, reaching incredible levels. Some were prepared to pay almost one million pounds for an F40. A 1963 version of the 250 GTO went to a collector for a staggering ten million pounds.

The market subsided just as quickly and unexpectedly at the beginning of the nineties. Desirable is normally only that which is scarce. But even the frequent presence of the speedy beauty on the world's roads cannot destroy the myth. Whereas over 1000 of these motorised works of art were built in 1971 for the first time, the production later rose to undreamt-of heights. 4236 vehicles were delivered to customers in 2002, besides a further 3300 Maseratis.

The former major rival, and no less legendary marque – one could say from the same neighbourhood – had incorporated Ferrari in 1997. A well used pitchfork keeps a stable spick and span. Apart from the formation of the Ferrari-Maserati group, President Luca di Montezemolo is subjecting his "empire" to a thorough overhaul. In Maranello modern, bright halls with generously calculated green spaces – even in production buildings – are arising on a total area of 232,000 square metres (57.3 acres). The coach building production in Modena and the entire environment of the Fiorano test track are experiencing the blessings of modernity. Even the track itself is not excluded. The worst rainstorm can be simulated in only a few minutes thanks to an innovative sprinkler system. And star architect Renzo Piano's new wind tunnel is capable of displaying all the behavioural effects of turbulent surroundings.

Montezemolo sums up the harmony of the production plants with the work of the people operating in them in his *Formula Uomo*. And for the wellbeing of

his employees he adds the *Formula Benessere* under the supervision of respected Italian Olympic selection doctors. This unique radical course of treatment requires an enormous financial potential. However, this is not a problem for the shareholders, among which are four banks. What does Ferrari vice president Piero Ferrari have in common with the German Commerzbank? Both hold ten per cent of the successful enterprise, the majority belongs to Fiat. Here, Montezemolo has been sitting on the board since 2003.

Ferrari's racetrack success story – also in the FIA GT Championship – is mirrored in the series production: inimitable treasures, magnificent powerhouses such as the Enzo and individual masterpieces. Nothing is impossible for the coachbuilder Scaglietti, which has devoted itself completely to the personal wishes of the Ferraristi. The norm is the *non plus ultra,* here and there with a *numerus clausus* applied – for example with the Enzo, limited to 399 vehicles.

Where the objects of desire are to be seen: the showroom of the new company complex at Maranello

Designed by the renowned architect Renzo Piano, and conceived by President Luca di Montezemolo as a great step forward: the new domicile combines high-tech with the Formula Benessere – a mixture that seems to function.

Ferrari

The Cars

Spider (Barchetta) Touring

Founded in 1926, Carrozzeria Touring did not take long to carve itself a solid reputation based on tradition; a fact that had not escaped Enzo Ferrari. In 1940 this mutual esteem, coupled with a common love of competition, led to a collaboration. Bianchi Anderloni, the boss of Touring, busied himself with dressing Ferrari's first creation, the Auto Avio Costruzioni Tipo 815.

But the auspicious start to their relationship was rudely interrupted by the Second World War and it was not until the Turin Motor Show in September 1948 that a new project was unveiled; the spider Touring 166 MM. These initials celebrated the winning of that year's Mille Miglia by Biondetti and Navone. It was soon called *Barchetta* or "little boat". This nimble little car was much talked about for the next five years, as much for its racing successes as for its fine lines. These were the result of following the *Superleggera* principle, perfected by Anderloni. On the frame itself was fitted a multi-tubular assembly that was then covered in sheets of pre-formed aluminium. These were in turn fitted to the mechanical components that Ferrari would have delivered to the company's Milan-based workshops at 65 Via Lodovico de Breme.

Despite its long model life, the Barchetta's silhouette remained pretty much the same. Under its curvaceous body, however, the twelve cylinder engines changed their cubic capacity from 166 to 340 cc per cylinder and therefore their model numbers. The 166 MM already developed 140 horsepower, while the 1950 version with its 4.1 litres put out 220 horsepower. Both versions were easily capable of over 200 km per hour (125 mph).

Appeared in September 1948: the Spider Touring 166 MM with its striking front and light aluminium bodywork, drawn by Touring boss Bianchi Anderloni

While the chassis bore even numbers to indicate their competition pedigree, several Touring spiders were destined for road use. For example this black 340 America trimmed in green leather, which was shown at the Paris Salon in October 1950 and served to increase the passion roused by Ferrari's work. Pleasing to the eye, it was also a feast for the ears. The robust V12 designed by Aurelio Lampredi employed a long block as used by the marque's racing units. It produced a sound which was every bit as emotive as

that produced by the short-block engines developed by Lampredi's colleague, Gioachino Colombo.

Still quoted by the AC Ace in 1953 and the Cobra in 1962, the aesthetic qualities of the Barchetta were often held up as being state of the art. In the meantime, the business arrangement between Ferrari and Touring had come to an end, without signifying the end of a solid friendship. As late as 1987, Carlo Felice Bianchi Anderloni would receive a letter from Maranello — a few polite words dictated by a legendary figure.

The small 166 Spider, also known as Barchetta (small boat), was very convincing with its flowing lines and balanced proportions. It weighed only 900 kilograms (1985 lbs).

An optical and aural pleasure: the twelve-cylinder aggregate with scarcely 2.6-litre capacity achieved 170 bhp with its three Weber carburetors.

Coupé Ghia

Without a doubt, the study of the code names and abbreviations that Ferrari attributed to his cars is a science in itself, and could be seen as the shorthand version of their history. Thus the addition of the word "Inter" to a model name indicated Ferrari's wish to finance his participation in competition from the profits from the sale of road-going Grand Tourers; thinly disguised racers that were a bit easier to tame.

To this end, the conquest of the American market was of major importance and the Carrozzeria Ghia was to play a catalytic role in this. Shortly before his death on 21st February 1944, the founder of this company, Giacinto Ghia, handed over the business to Mario Felice Boano. Boano and his son, Gian Paolo had a good relationship with the Chrysler company for whom they had built dream cars like the K310.

However the relationship with Ferrari was short and relatively unproductive. The work of Boano lacked that touch of genius displayed by Giovanni Michelotti, who worked for rival coachbuilder Vignale.

The white berlinetta built onto the chassis of the 166 Inter of 1950 was followed a year later by ten

195 Inters. Boano commissioned his son-in-law Ezio Ellena to build these, as his own business, based on Via Tommaso Grossi in Turin, was overloaded with work. In 1952, ten (though some say twelve) 212 Inters and five 340 Americas, as well as three Ghia cabriolets – the only ones built on chassis supplied by Ferrari – were to signal the end of this collaboration. Vignale was the first to benefit from this parting of the ways.

Ghia's clients included the popular racer Gigi Villoresi as well as King Farouk of Egypt, already delighted with his Boano-bodied Rolls-Royce.

A rare appearance: the Ferrari 195 Inter was kitted out by Carrozzeria Ghia in Turin. It is said that only ten models were produced.

Coupé Ghia

Typical elements: many Italian coupés of the early fifties were produced with right-hand drive, just as characteristic was the sumptuous chrome work on the console, or the subtle, almost suggested, tail fins.

Spider Vignale

Ferrari's first ten years in business coincided with a period of strong creativity in Italian design, which led to some interesting and important collaborations. To style a Ferrari, especially a winning one, was the surest way to hit the headlines.

Alfredo Vignale knew how to play this game. The Ferrari 340 America, the 250 Sport and 340 MM which won the Mille Miglia from 1951 to 1953, the 212 Inter Coupé which Piero Taruffi and Luigi Chinetti drove to victory in the 1951 Carrera Panamericana, as well as four of the five Ferraris entered for the 1952 Monaco Grand Prix which that year was a sports car race, were all cars with Vignale bodywork.

The relationship between Enzo Ferrari and Carrozzeria Vignale, situated in the Vanchiglietta district of Turin was established in the spring of 1950 thanks to the efforts of a wealthy Milan car dealer, Franco Cornacchia, who acted as intermediary. The relationship prospered for five years, starting with a 166 MM coupé, designed in the summer of 1950. Its last collaboration in 1968 led to the production of a remarkable vehicle, a shooting brake based on a 330 GT 2+2.

The creative genius at Alfredo Vignale was none other than his friend Giovanni Michelotti, whose ideas he translated into reality using a very original method. First of all, Michelotti's designs were transposed into 1:1 scale drawings on sheets of aluminium which were then attached to wooden bucks and hammered into rough shape. The final curvature was obtained using the same method, except over sacks of sand this time. The pieces of bodywork thus produced were then fixed to a metal skeleton using screws and rivets. Then a primer coating was applied before the final procedure of painting was undertaken by Alfredo's brother, Guglielmo.

The entire operation was a cottage industry. All Vignale's creations inevitably lacked symmetry and there was absolutely no question of running a production line. Vignale and Michelotti would steer clear of anything remotely monotonous. Their virtuosity extended from the truly classical to the excessively baroque, and when the need arose they were not afraid of delving into the style of art deco. Their sometimes over-fertile imagination produced bodywork for 155 Ferrari chassis. These were characterised

Light elegance: the 166 MM, bodywork by the Vignale designer Giovanni Michelotti, inspired with its functional elegance. The film director Roberto Rossellini and King Leopold of Belgium both drove Ferraris with Vignale bodywork.

by oblong or round air intakes, scoops with no function, fussy door handles, the whole thing sprinkled with chrome.

The celebrities of the day appreciated this overblown style. Vignale produced Ferraris for the film director Roberto Rossellini; Leopold III, King of Belgium; Prince Bernard of the Netherlands; the elegant British actor David Niven and his feisty colleague, Anna Magnani; as well as Porfirio Rubirosa, whose playboy image was enhanced by his ownership of a Ferrari until he died at the wheel.

The Ferrari 195 Inter with its Vignale bodywork also had a delicate and elegant appearance. The filigree door handles were typical for Vignale creations of the time.

250 MM Coupé Pinin Farina

"**E**ither I win the Mille Miglia or I die in the attempt." A heavy smoker and temperamental, Giovanni Bracco was not in the habit of eating his words. He accepted his own challenge and won the event in atrocious conditions in May 1952. His car was an experimental Ferrari 250 S fitted with a short stroke engine prepared by Gioachino Colombo. For this event he had fitted cylinder heads similar to those used by Aurelio Lampredi on the larger capacity factory cars. The bodywork was by Vignale, with modifications by Francesco Salomone, a stylist at Pinin Farina before the prototype was displayed at the Geneva Motor Show in March 1953. This was to lead to the production of a coupé called the 250 MM built to honour Bracco's win. Seventeen more examples were built as well as fourteen spiders, although not all were signed Farina.

The 250 MM was compact and manoeuvrable, mainly thanks to its short 2400 mm (7'10") wheelbase. It was notable more for its agility than for its speed. The factory claimed a top speed of 255 km per hour (159 mph), which put it far behind the 375 MM which was capable of 298 km per hour (185 mph). Unlike the first prototype, the gearbox had four synchromesh gears rather than five crash gears. Its performance level meant the 250 MM was by no means a competition beast but it was much appreciated all the same.

On the road it had the advantage of being easy to drive; as confirmed by a journalist for *Sports Car and Lotus Owner* magazine who tested the car in May 1957. On a quiet Sunday morning driving from Hampstead to Kingston through the deserted streets of London, the writer passengered Mackay Frazer, a driver with the Lotus team who owned a 250 MM which already had 36,000 kms (22,500 miles) on the

The father of innumerable victories: the legendary twelve-cylinder engine with its three-litre capacity was first used in the 250 MM (Mille Miglia) which dominated international motor sport in the fifties. Its first victory: the Mille Miglia of 1952.

clock. On the return journey Frazer let the journalist take the wheel, who admitted to enjoying the best motoring experience of his life, when, at 144 km per hour (90 mph) and with the engine spinning at 6000 rpm, he changed up from third to fourth!

Equally impressive was the braking. At this speed it needed only 130 metres (140 yards) to stop as it approached traffic lights which were turning red. The 250 MM stopped with all the style of a jet fighter on an aircraft carrier. In the report, the author also remembered the look of surprise on the petrol pump attendant's face as he poured in 220 litres (58 gallons) of fuel.

The large panoramic rear window was characteristic of the 250MM fashioned by Battista Pinin Farina. Three Weber double carburetors provided the twelve cylinders with the right mixture of fuel and air.

250 GT Europa Pinin Farina

250 GT Europa Pinin Farina

The two models displayed on the stand of Ferrari importer, Autoval, at the Paris Salon in October 1953 were as similar as two peas in a pod. They were imposing vehicles with high waistlines and narrow windows.

The differences were to be found mainly under the bonnet. Those who were familiar with Ferrari's model numbers would have known this. Fitted with a 4.5 litre engine, the 375 GT America was reserved for the United States, while the 2963 cc version, the 250 Europa, was destined for the Old World where big engines were more heavily taxed.

The two units were based on the Lampredi engine, the Europa having a perfectly square engine with a bore and stroke of 68 mm and a power output between 200 and 220 willing horses. There are no available road test reports of the day, but today this model is considered as a strong car with rather heavy steering.

14 of the 18 chassis built between September 1953 and July 1954 had bodywork by Pinin Farina. Added to this were 27 of a batch of 44 second generation cars built up to January 1956. These were initially christened Europa but the name was later changed to the simple GT. The GT was presented once again in Paris at the traditional autumn show in 1954. It was almost identical to the previous model. However, Farina did offer two variants, one with a panoramic curved rear window and the other with a flat rear screen and two triangular side windows.

All in all, the models in the second series appeared more compact and better balanced, as the

The filigree greenhouse lent the 250 GT Europa the elegance that distinguished this Gran Turismo by Battista Pinin Farina.

result of admittedly drastic surgical measures which were a definite improvement. The exceptionally long 2800 mm (9'2") wheelbase had been shortened by 200 mm (8"), as the chassis was built to take the shorter Colombo-designed engine; its 2953 cc putting out 240 horsepower. The stroke remained the same at 58.8 mm, unchanged since 1948, but the bore had now been increased to 73 mm.

The central beam of the chassis was bent in such a way as to straddle the rear axle; at the front helical springs replaced the previous transverse leaf spring. The cockpit dimensions remained unchanged, which did nothing to improve comfort. But after all, that was part of the undeniable charm that was included in the sale price of every Ferrari.

The small indicators in front of the panoramic rear window, the round fog lights by Marchal, and the cylinder head covers embellished with black wrinkle paint, were all in keeping with the Zeitgeist of the mid 50s.

375 MM Spider · 375 Plus

The 375 MM Spider Competizione was an immediate success. In December 1953, in the hands of Nino Farina and Piero Scotti, it won the 12 Hours of Casablanca at its first time of asking. It was clothed in thin sheets of Peraluman alloy fixed to a chrome molybdenum steel structure. Form followed function perfectly without suffering any aerodynamic constraints.

The 375 MM, which was the biggest sports car in the range so far, went into the history books as a rugged beast, noisy and shaking with power. The original version resembled an elongated 250 MM coupé. On 13th and 14th June of 1953, in the hands of Alberto Ascari and Gigi Villoresi, it survived until dawn on the Le Mans circuit. Without batting an eyelid, its mechanics claimed the engine was identical to the one used for Ferrari's Indy project in 1952. Indeed, many believed an identical engine had already been fitted to Giannino Marzotto's 340 MM which won the Mille Miglia that April. This would

certainly have given him a distinct advantage as this car was listed as having a 4.1 litre engine.

With the 375 MM, Ferrari won the 24 Hours of Spa in July followed by the 1000 Kilometres at the Nürburgring in August, which meant he had taken a big step towards the 1953 Constructors' title.

The Farina spider was specifically aimed at the booming private customer market. Each car was unique: some had cutaway fenders, some headrests or vertical fins integrated into the rear bodywork.

There was at least one version which was never seen on the racetrack. It was chassis number 0460 AM, and was distinguished by its yellow paintwork, its green leather interior, its flat windscreen, and its tiny vertically mounted bumpers. In 1954 it was sold to one Mrs. Day in the USA and from that moment it was cosseted and pampered like a piece of the finest silverware.

However, the 375 Plus was not destined to be treated with the same mollycoddled kindness. As

The 375 Plus was the winning type. With it, Ferrari won the Spa 24 Hour race and the Nürburgring 1000 Kilometres in 1953.

factory cars, they were sold off cheaply at the end of the 1954 season. With 344 horsepower on tap they only had four horsepower in hand over the 375 MM, but thanks to their de Dion rear axle, they were much better balanced and had superior road holding. They proved their superiority by winning two of the three most spectacular endurance races of the day, the Le Mans 24 Hours in June with Froilán Gonzalez and Maurice Trintignant and the Carrera Panamericana in November with Umberto Maglioli.

The aluminium tank dominated the trunk while the powerful twelve-cylinder aggregate achieved 345 bhp with its five-litre capacity.

750 Monza

In the 1950 season a troublemaker arrived to put into question Enzo Ferrari's almost immutable faith in the virtues of the twelve cylinder engine. The master strategist whose convictions were shared by his faithful Maranello courtiers had been impressed by the performances of the Englishman Stirling Moss at the wheel of his fellow countryman John Heath's HWM. All the more so because this car was powered by a four cylinder Alta engine.

So in the winter of 1951/52, Ferrari asked Aurelio Lampredi to build a four cylinder unit. The aim was to obtain better torque, and it worked according to plan with only four ratios in the gearbox being quite sufficient at the majority of race tracks. Comparatively reasonable fuel consumption of 22 to 24 litres per 100 kilometres (11 to 10 mpg) and approximately ten more horsepower than the 166 engine were just some of the other advantages.

This was to prove the cornerstone which would enable Alberto Ascari to have unchallenged superiority in the 1952 and 1953 World Championships which, according to the rules, were fought out between two litre Formula 2 cars. To his credit went two world titles and eleven wins – nine of them in succession – from fifteen starts.

However, when compared to this glittering and glorious record, the sports cars used by Ferrari, based

A riveted wooden steering wheel with aluminium spokes, and five instruments – the cockpit of the 750 Monza was limited to the basics.

on these Formula 2 machines from 1953, had a distinctly dull time. One of these versions was the 750 Monza, of which three were built by Pinin Farina, and a further 27 by Scaglietti from a sketch produced by Enzo Ferrari's son Dino. The 2999 cc engine had been pushed to the three litre limit maximum capacity rule. It put out 260 horsepower and reliability was not its strong point. At first the gearbox had five ratios but this was later changed to four without synchromesh. It was mated to the differential on the de Dion rear axle.

The 750 Monza came up against stiff competition, including the twelve cylinder cars of the same marque, but above all from the Mercedes 300 SLR. The Belgian racer and journalist, Paul Frère, went so far as to consider the 750 Monza a failure, describing it as "a plank of wood with four wheels and an impressive power unit". There was a reason for this assessment. Paul Frère drove a 750 Monza, in the colours of the Belgian National Team, in the 1955 Swedish Grand Prix. It was there, under the sceptical eye of Ferrari's Sporting Director Nello Ugolini, that he had the misfortune to go off the road when his car reared up on the bumpy track like some reluctant stallion. Paul Frère came to in a field, his leg broken, before being taken to hospital in Kristianstad.

Paul Frère recalled that the car had recalcitrant steering and useless brakes. To cap it all it would understeer wickedly. These reflections led him to believe that the car's handling may have been the cause of the mysterious fatal accident that claimed the life of Alberto Ascari on 26th May 1955, at a corner of the Monza track that, to this day, is named after the great Italian driver.

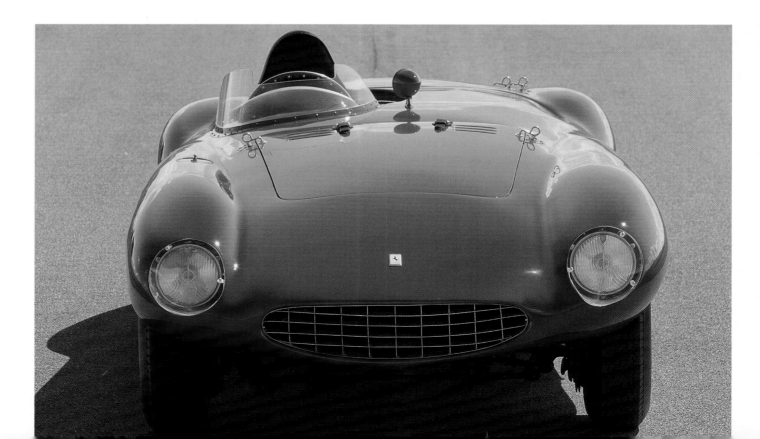

The hump behind the driver optimized the aerodynamics, the four-cylinder motor with its three-litre capacity managed 250 bhp, however, the big success failed to materialize.

51

Variations on a theme:
The powerful 410 S was
built in Maranello as both
a spider and as a coupé.

The two Scaglietti Type 410 Sports were the ultimate, both visually and technically. They were originally built to compete in the sixth running of the Carrera Panamerica which was lost from the calendar forever. Their engine was closely related to that of the 410 Superamerica, equipped like that of the 375 F1 of 1951, with 24 sparking plugs; a second row having been squeezed in on the exhaust side of the head. Their de Dion axle also represented a step towards the future.

But they had a delicate constitution and were, in a word, fragile. This was proved in their only official race appearance, on 19th January 1956 at the Buenos Aires 1000 Kilometres, despite the fact that they had the best possible driver line-up of the day. Juan Manuel Fangio and Eugenio Castellotti were in one car and Luigi Musso and Peter Collins were entrusted with the other. The cars were remarkably quick, hitting a top speed of 303.5 kph (188.6 mph), and on this hybrid track that used part of the Autodromo Municipal and the Avenida General Paz, Peter Collins set a new lap record.

But shortly after that, both cars developed problems with the rear axle. Stirling Moss and Carlos Menditeguy won the event in a Maserati 300 S, Phil Hill and Olivier Gendebien were second in a Ferrari 860 Monza, which from then on would play an ever more important role for the Maranello marque.

The 410 S's were quickly sold, and one of them went to the United States, where it was used in national events by drivers like John Elgar and Joakim Bonnier. Its sister car was bought by the Swede, Sture Nottorp, who never achieved anything of note with it. Two more 410 S's were built with a conventional spark plug arrangement. One was another spider, while the second was a coupé, specially commissioned by Michel Paul Cavalier, a close friend of the Commendatore and boss of a French gearbox company. He later became a director of SEFAC. Cavalier was not a fan of off-the-peg cars, and had the knack of distinguishing the simply unusual from the completely exceptional.

Ferrari obtained the classical round instruments from Jaeger. Three Weber double carburetors took care of preparing the mixture for the 380 bhp-strong twelve cylinders.

The large aluminium tank, placed over the rear axle, was a handmade masterpiece. Several hundred rivets were set by hand, and the aluminium honed also by hand.

410 Superamerica Series I
410 Superamerica Series II
410 Superamerica Series III

This was an *à la carte* Ferrari, made to measure for America in the fifties; for people who wanted to express their social status through their cars. Without being blatant, the 410 SA was all the same imposing and provocative and was produced in three batches, totalling 37 cars, all with minor differences but still basically the same car. The common denominator was the superb 4962 cc engine, which at first developed 340 horsepower and later 360. The long-block V12 reached its apotheosis in this car, although Aurelio Lampredi had already left the company in 1955. The engine and chassis assembly had been shown under the artificial lights of the Paris Salon in 1955. But the coupé was not seen for the first time until the Brussels show in January 1956. The family connection to the Boano 250 GT was apparent, but it was more generously proportioned and had finer lines. Twelve months later a second version saw the light of day. It was built on a chassis that was 200 mm (8") shorter, but only the barest possible difference was noticeable in the doors.

Unveiled in 1958 in Paris, where it was much admired, the third-generation Superamerica had several modifications. The brakes were a different size, the track had been widened by 100 mm (4"), and the engine, whose spark plugs were located above the branches of the exhaust manifold, could not hide the fact that it was the child of the Testa Rossa engine. Its lines, flowing and smooth, were timeless. Its headlights were either tucked in behind oval covers or sat in the tops of the wings.

By the end of 1959, by which time the last Superamerica was on its way to New York, the concept and design of almost all Ferraris was in the hands of Pinin Farina.

This model had given birth to a series of strange cars, including this red coupé from the pen of Mario Savonuzzi, chief designer at Ghia. It was charac-

The striking air scoop and the lattice grill characterized many Ferraris of the time.

In no way does the interior spoil with sumptuous luxury. The front ventilation grill and light tail fins were reminiscent of the American market.

terised by fins on the rear sides and enormous curves. Pinin Farina himself produced two Superfast versions. The first of these was the star of the 1956 Paris Salon. Fitted with a 24 spark plug engine and white-blue bodywork, it was elaborately styled and represented the master coachbuilder's ideal of the American Dream.

The second version, shorter by 120 mm (4¾") and 50 mm (2") higher, had a distinctly more European look about it. In the spring of 1958, its owner, Jan de Vroom, who along with Luigi Chinetti and George Arents was one of the key figures in the North American Racing Team, was brave enough to entrust this unique creation to the road tester from *Sports Car Illustrated.* This gentleman started by terrifying the innocent driver of an MG TF, by making the engine howl until he overtook him on the Hutchinson River Parkway in New York. Then he recorded the best ever test figures seen by the magazine, including those for racing cars: acceleration from 0 to 60 mph (96 kph) in 5.6 seconds, with the 100 mph barrier (160 kph) coming up in a mere 12.1 seconds. The reporter also noted that it was possible to break all the speed limits enforced in the USA in first gear, whereas even at only 800 rpm in fourth gear the car would accelerate strongly without stuttering. He concluded by comparing the car to a woman, who if she gave her all, had the right to expect respect in return!

250 GT Boano/Ellena

Unveiled at the Geneva Motor Show in March 1956, along with a 250 Boano GT and a 410 Superamerica by Pinin Farina, the precursor of a new generation of Ferraris appeared rather massive: only small areas of glass, an imposing cockpit, a strong horizontal line and a truncated rear which flattered the boot. The oval radiator grille took its inspiration from the 118 and 121 LM models and incorporated in each end were two fog lights. The engine was based on Colombo's three litre unit which had powered the 1952 Mille Miglia winning 250 S.

Before going into the history books as the first Ferrari produced in bigger numbers, the 250 GT would go through two further changes. Pinin Farina, responsible for the prototype, was planning to move his business to Grugliasco, on the outskirts of Turin. It was a bigger site chosen by his son Sergio and son-in-law, Renzo Carli. The only condition he imposed was that it had to have a view of the Alps and some trees in the foreground. It was here that Mario Felice Boano was given the job of producing a run of the new coupés. But first he allowed himself to make some aesthetic changes, in particular removing the kick-up behind the doors. In January 1958 the writers on the American magazine *Sports Car Illustrated,* could not conceal their enthusiasm for this car, of which Boano produced 75. They reckoned it was sensibly priced at US$ 10,975. However, they were not so impressed with the odd gear selection pattern: third and fourth gears were between reverse gear and first and second gears.

A filigree masterpiece for the rearview: the elegantly curved rearview mirror of the 250 GT Boano.

Although it had been partly civilized, the 250 GT lost none of its spirit. Richie Ginther proved that by winning the first ever race for GT cars on the East Coast, at Lime Rock, in the actual car used for the magazine's road test.

In the spring of 1957, Boano joined Fiat as chief stylist. He left his partner Luciano Pollo and his son-in-law Ezio Ellena in charge of his business on the Via Collegno, now to become Carrozzeria Ellena.

Their version of the 250 GT appeared at the Turin Motor Show in November 1957, although some had already been sold. Compared to the previous version, modifications were minimal: the brakes and windows were bigger, the quarterlights on the side windows had been removed, boot capacity had increased by positioning the spare wheel under the floor, and the boot itself had been shortened. 49 customers had the pleasure of owning this version.

A total of 49 250 GT Boanos were produced in the halls of the coachbuilders on the Via Collegno of Turin in 1957.

250 GT Tour de France

The 1956 250 GT was a rapid and decisive response to a psychological and technical challenge. Firstly, in 1955, Armando Zampiero had won the Italian Sports Car Championship at the wheel of a Mercedes 300 SL, a real insult in the kingdom of the *cavallino rampante*. Secondly it was a response to a new regulation introduced by the Fédération Internationale de l'Automobile for GT cars, as a result of the tragic accident at Le Mans in 1955, when 86 people, apart from Mercedes driver Pierre Levegh had been killed.

After the groundwork had been done with the building of two prototypes, the 250 GT in its provisionally definitive form was shown at the Geneva Motor Show in March 1956. Pinin Farina had sketched the outline and nearly all the cars were

built by the Scaglietti concern in Modena, after they had fine-tuned the concept delivered to them by the Turin master coachbuilder.

Even if the odd numbers allocated to the chassis indicated that this fastback berlinetta was a road-going sports car, it was nevertheless a thoroughbred Ferrari. Even with 130 litres (34 gallons) of fuel on board, it weighed only 1160 kilos (2560 lbs), while its

The prototype of the Pinin Farina 250 GT received its première in 1956. The 250-model range was soon very much in demand, and that internationally. Ferrari built many diverse model variations of this range up until 1964 – including this later variation.

Characteristic of the 250 GT TdF (Tour de France) were, apart from the 2.60-metre (8'6") wheelbase, the side air outlets behind the doors.

cockpit, as spartan as a monk's cell, could not be accused of adding to the driving pleasure.

Its evolution went through five successive phases, some of which drew on the original concept. The three litre engine from the pen of Gioachino Colombo grew steadily from 240 to 260 horsepower.

At the rear, the height and shape of the line above the wheels went through several changes. At first the lights were positioned at the outer edges of the car, behind a small circle of chrome no wider than an inch. Later they were placed further back in the extension of the wings, before eventually returning to their original position. While in the initial stages of production the panoramic rear window extended to the sides, from November 1956 this design was abolished. The rear window adopted a more conventional shape, whereas the sides consisted of a panel with fourteen

openings, later reduced to three and then one. This panel was made of aluminium just like the rest of the bodywork.

The 250 GT lived up to expectations in exemplary fashion. Many of its successes are linked to the name of the Belgian racing driver, Olivier Gendebien: fifth overall and first in class in the 1957 Mille Miglia; third overall and first in class in the same event the following year, accompanied on both occasions by his fellow countryman Jacques Washer: two outright wins in the 12 Hours of Reims in 1957 and 1958, with Paul Frère; three outright victories in the overall classification of the Tour de France from 1957 to 1959, with yet another Belgian co-driver, Lucien Bianchi.

The 250 GT acquired its battle honours and hence its name of Tour de France from these performances as well as from the achievements of the Spanish Marquis, Alfonso de Portago, and his American friend Edmund Nelson, who won this great French classic event as early as 1956.

The three-litre aggregate achieved in the TdF 260 bhp at 7000 rpm, while the tank, sealed by an aluminium cap, held 130 litres (34½ gallons) of fuel.

500 Testa Rossa
500 TRC
250 TR
TR 59
TR 60
TR 61
TR 62

The name Testa Rossa is synonymous with some of the most memorable successes in the history of the Ferrari marque. It was called "red head" because the cam covers which adorned the cylinder heads were painted red. What is more, these cars caused the opposition to turn red with embarrassment when they met in competition. Its role of honour includes 13 particularly important wins, as well as the World Championships in 1958, 1960 and 1961. This run was only interrupted in 1959 by Aston Martin, with the aid of some God-given luck and a driving genius by the name of Stirling Moss. At that time the Testa Rossa project was already three years old, as it had begun in 1956 with the two litre 500 TR version, its 190 horsepower 4 cylinder unit produced by engine builder Alberto Massimino. At the end of 1956 appeared the TRC, which Ferrari used to tackle the demands of Appendix C of the sporting regulations, even if this had certain elements that did not seem reasonable: a passenger door, a full-width windscreen, a folding roof and a spare wheel. As was the case with the TR, the bodywork was designed by Pinin Farina and built by Scaglietti. The entire production run was bought by very satisfied customers.

The 250 Testa Rossa appeared in 1957 and the project chief was Carlo Chiti, who anticipated things to come as, from 1958, the regulations limited the engine capacity for sports cars to three litres. Ferrari therefore perfected its armoury by taking the chassis from the 290 MM, the power unit from the 250 GT,

Nomen ist omen: *red-painted cylinder head covers (testa rossa = red head) embellished the engines of this model range. It began with the 500 TR with its four cylinders and two-litre capacity.*

and the bodywork of the TR. Two prototypes ran in the Nürburgring 1000 Kilometres and the 24 Hours of Le Mans, affording a glimpse of the Testa Rossa's potential. Then, at a press conference held on 22nd November 1957, Enzo Ferrari launched the production version with its characteristic spectacular cutaway fenders, designed to cool the huge drum brakes, a four speed synchromesh box and the magical power output of 100 horsepower per litre. It was destined for the Californian Ferrari concessionaire, John von Neumann.

Once again from the pen of Pinin Farina and built by Medardo Fantuzzi, the TR 59 was more compact. It had a five speed box and disc brakes with an engine

that pumped out 306 horsepower. In 1960, as stipu-lated by the regulations, the windscreen was 25 cm (10") high, the boot lid was longer, and some versions, identified with the model number TRI, had indepen-dent suspension.

The TRI 61 showed some similarities with the Dino 156 F1 single-seater. It was easily recognizable by its radiator grille with two apertures and its rear spoiler. The last Testa Rossa appeared in 1962. It was a 330 TRI/LM powered by a 360 horsepower four litre engine. It was entered for the 24 Hours of Le Mans with Phil Hill and Olivier Gendebien driving; just one against the rest. And it won, signing off as a magnificent postscript to what had been a grand era.

The 500 TRC appeared at the end of 1956, the bodywork was manufactured by Scaglietti in Modena, and the four-cylinder engine with its two overhead camshafts achieved 190 bhp.

500 Testa Rossa · 500 TRC · 250 TR · TR 59 · TR 60 · TR 61 · TR 62

The 500 TR was almost unbeatable in sports car racing of the second half of the 1950s.

(Overleaf) The historic dream automobile at a race in England: the 1958 250 TR is already in starting position. A little later Phil Hill gets behind the steering wheel of the 3-litre 12-cylinder to win the race.

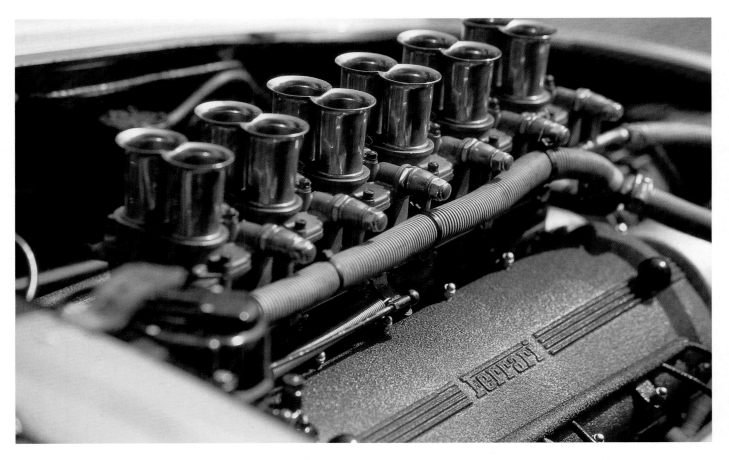

The deep recesses behind the front wheels for cooling the brake drums were typical of the 250 Testa Rossa of 1958.

Phil Hill and Olivier
Gendebien won the
prestigious Le Mans
24 hours in the 330 TRI.
A 360 bhp V12 engine
was on operation under
the hood.

290 S
315 S
335 S

More than any other Ferrari model number, this abbreviation – 335 S – made up of three numbers and a single letter sums up the highs and lows of motor sport. And both ends of the spectrum were reflected on the same day.

On 12th May 1957, at the wheel of one of these machines, Piero Taruffi, then aged 51, won the very last Mille Miglia. No sooner had he crossed the finish line, than his wife reminded him of the promise he had made to hang up his helmet forever. At the same moment, his team mate de Portago's 335 S had run its race not far from Brescia, leaving a tell-tale skid mark peppered with rubber, as it lay in a dark ditch, a pathetic tangle of steel and aluminium. In the course of that fatal race de Portago took with him to the grave his American co-driver Ed Nelson, as well as ten spectators, innocent bystanders at the side of the road.

In 1957 the marque's sports cars were fitted with four overhead camshafts. They had been developed by a team of engineers made up of Jano, Massimino, Bellantani and Fraschetti, who had combined elements of the Lampredi and Colombo engines used in the 290 MM. At first there was the 290 S, putting out 330 horsepower, which only ran once, in January's 1000 Kilometres of Buenos Aires. There followed the

In this cockpit Piero Taruffi steered the 335 S to the Mille Miglia victory on 12 May 1957. His team colleague de Portago suffered a fatal accident in his 335 S in the same race.

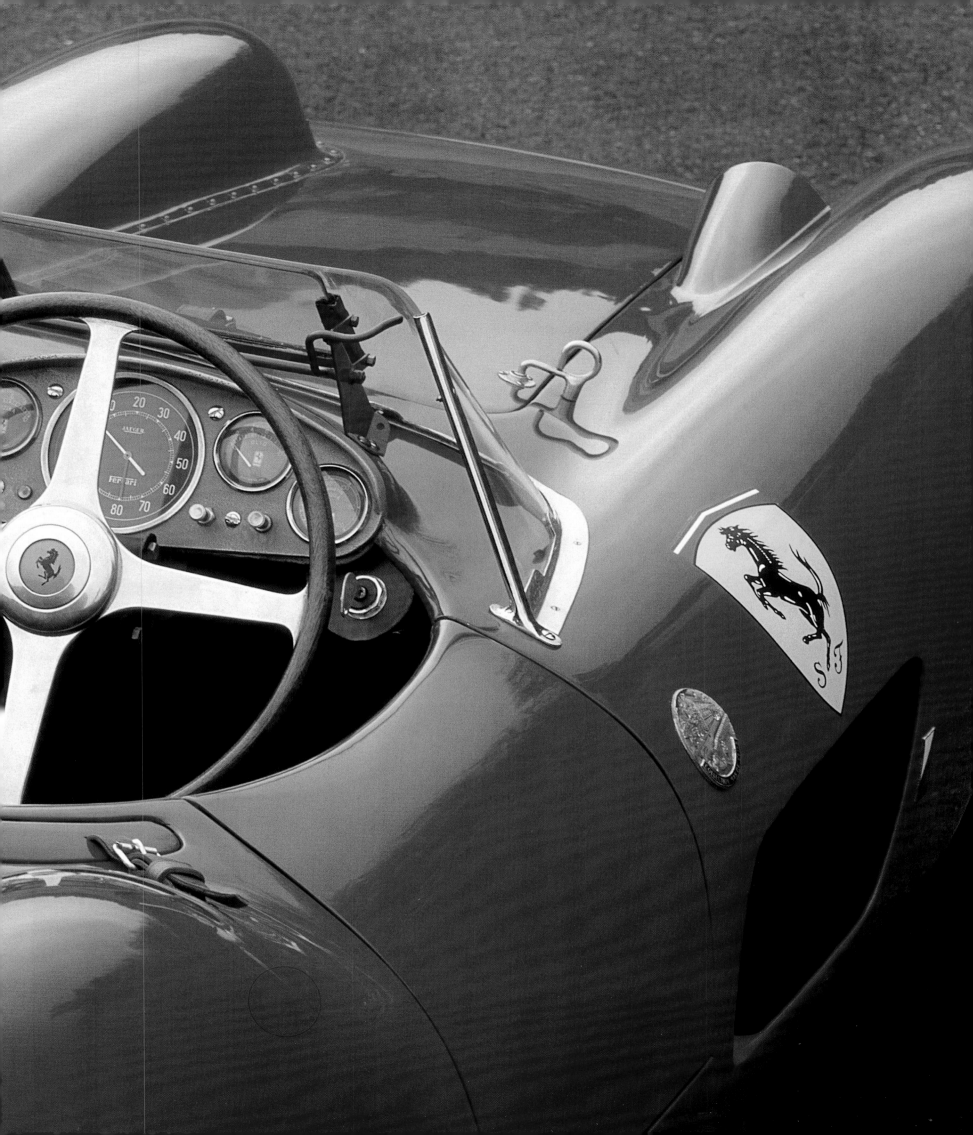

360 horsepower 315 S, with a considerably increased cubic capacity, which made its racing debut at Sebring in March. Then came the 335 S which at first produced 390 horsepower. Taruffi's win in the Mille Miglia was to prove to be a swallow that did not quite make a spring. When it went the distance, the Maserati 450 S was much too quick, while the four privately entered Jaguars at Le Mans, which finished ahead of the 315 S of Lewis-Evans/Severi, were far superior.

A quadruple success in Caracas, with two 335 S's ahead of two Testa Rossas, guaranteed Ferrari the world title, albeit in sad circumstances; the track was littered with broken Maseratis, some in flames, to the extent that the company was on the brink of collapse.

The large lattice grill of the 335 gives it an aggressive appearance; in general, however, the Pinin Farina creation is considered elegant and balanced in form.

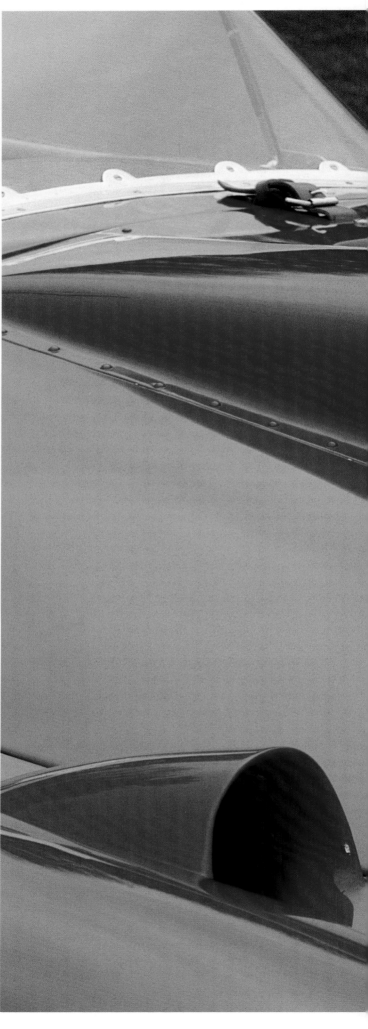

The six Weber type 42 DCN carburetors are responsible for preparing the mix for the 390 bhp twelve-cylinder aggregate with four-litre capacity.

250 GT Cabriolet Series I
250 GT Cabriolet Series II

Strangely enough the Ferrari 250 GT Cabriolet suffered a similar fate to the BMW 503 cabriolet and at roughly the same time. While the much prettier 507 put the 503 in the shade, the California Spyder, reckoned to be a much better car, eclipsed the 250 GT Cabriolet.

After several years typified by a certain reticence towards the cabriolet idea, Ferrari and Farina meticulously prepared their campaign in this sector of the market. At the 1957 Geneva Motor Show they introduced a red prototype whose most distinguishing feature was the nearside door, which sported a cutout found on several English roadsters. The man who had nonchalantly accepted the pleasure of getting his hands on it was none other than Ferrari's official driver, Peter Collins. The Commendatore had placed the car at his disposal with all the conditions normally attached to a company car. As a point of interest, at the time it was collected it had been painted British Racing Green.

Later, this charming cutout in the door was abolished and the car went on to play a pioneering role. In fact Collins fitted it with Dunlop disc brakes previously tested on a Testa Rossa, track standard from 1959 onwards, and adopted on production cars from 1960. It would take a further three models to predate the arrival of the 250 GT Cabriolet, as was its official name. Comprising a body made entirely of steel, its design was based on the Boano and Ellena coupé in what could be seen as a rather heavy-handed fashion. It was not dissimilar to its spider rival, which could not and would not deny its sporting background.

The 250 GT Cabriolet, designed and built once again by Pinin Farina of course, is considered one of the most beautiful automobiles of its time.

It was rapidly changed. Shown at the Paris Salon of 1959, the second series Cabriolet in terms of its shape and mechanical components obviously took its inspiration from the new Farina 250 GT coupé.

The concept allowed glimpses of the last of the old versions in that it was characterised by straight lines. The whole leaned towards luxury, comfort and pleasant journeys. For one, the engine had spark plugs on the outside of the cylinder heads which improved longevity and simplified maintenance. Double ignition and four speed gearbox with electrically-operated overdrive and disc brakes added to the effect. Modifications to the bodywork simply confirmed this move; a taller windscreen with less rake; quarterlights and bigger side windows; more room inside, a bigger boot and an attractive line for the hood, which from 1960 could be replaced with a removable hardtop.

Refinement and practicality. That is what this car was supposed to deliver, and it did.

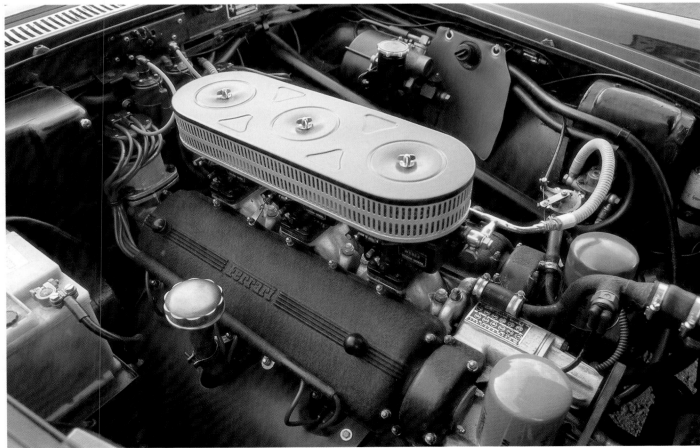

The long front and scantily cut cockpit are of classical proportions. Six unadorned round instruments inform the driver of the wellbeing of the optically impressive twelve-cylinder engine.

250 GT California Spyder Series I
250 GT California Spyder SWB

A request sent by the North American Ferrari concessionaires to Italy in 1957 resulted in a spectacular event: beauty on demand. A cabriolet based on the Berlinetta, this was their express wish. It had to be a light car, both agile and perfectly adapted to a land where the sun shone long and often. The result was the California Spyder, deliberately spelt with a "y". A prototype in 1957, it went into production in May 1958.

In fact it was pretty much a copy of the Granturismo coupé, give or take a few differences: a taller wind-screen, and in line with what marketing men know to be psychologically important, the silhouette resembled the female form.

Farina had sketched out the plans on his drawing board and Scaglietti had transformed them into reality.

But, as was the custom, one version was not enough. Although it bordered on perfection it would undergo several changes. Externally these would be merely cosmetic and often in response to customers' requests: headlights, uncovered or shielded behind

plexiglass, modifications to the rear lights and to the boot lid, and – occasionally – no side vents.

Some changes were not immediately apparent, however, but were hidden underneath the thin steel body of the Spyder, although the doors and bonnet were actually made out of light alloy. At the end of 1959 the drum brakes were replaced by Dunlop discs and the spark plugs were repositioned outside the V of the twelve cylinder engine, as on the Testa Rossa.

The first example of the second series Spyder appeared at the 1960 Geneva show. It was a derivative

The 250 GT California Spyder owes its existence to the initiative of American Ferrari dealers. With its unity of form, it is today still considered one of the Pinin Farina design icons.

of the contemporary Berlinetta SWB, although any similarity had been disguised. The wheelbase had been reduced by 200 mm (8") to 2400 mm (7'10"), while at the same time the front and rear track had been increased thus making it look wider and lower. Adjustable telescopic dampers had replaced Houdaille torsion bars at the front and new cylinder-heads gave an increase in power which in time rose from 250 to 280 horsepower. The car remained in this form until the final units were delivered to the United States in 1963.

Some versions were built entirely of aluminium, others were fitted with genuine competition engines, while some had both. One of these even finished fifth at Le Mans in 1959, giving its crew of Bob Grossman and Fernand Tavano no cause to regret their choice. Nothing strange in this, as the majority of California Spyder owners were convinced that, if they wanted to, they could do the same, although they felt that their beautiful car was far too precious to abuse in this fashion.

Apart from the seven instruments providing information, the cockpit offers no optical highpoint. Four forward gears can be engaged by the 250 GT pilot using the hefty gear leaver.

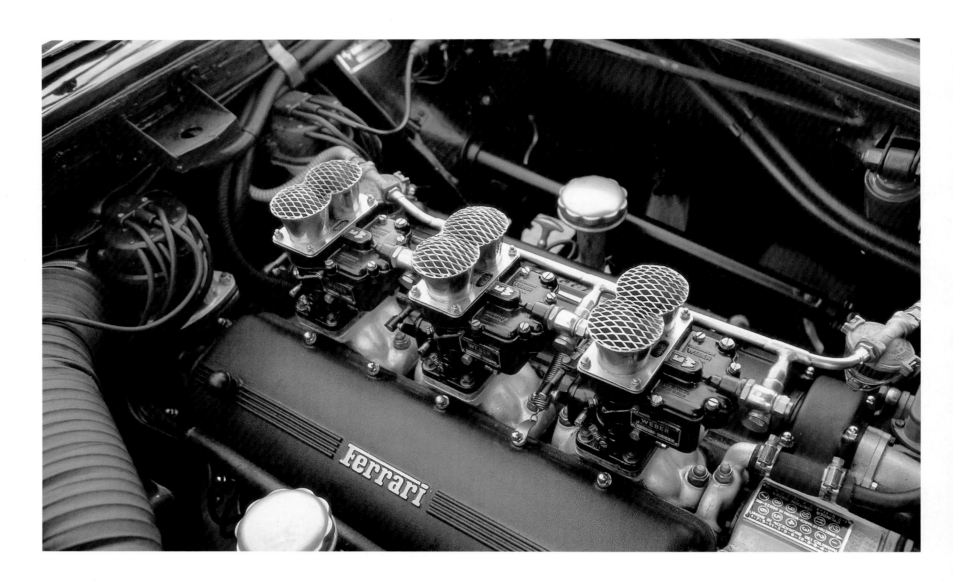

250 GT California Spyder Series I, 250 GT California Spyder SWB

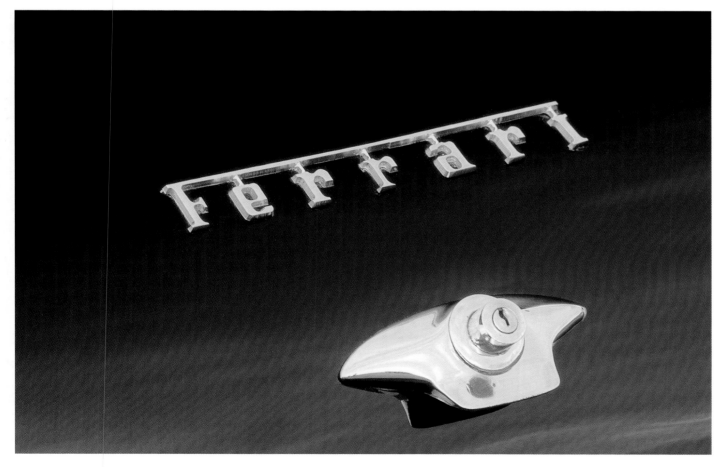

The California Spyder silhouette bewitches from every point of view, while, under the hood, the three-litre engine with its three double Weber carburetors provides a feast for the eyes.

The layout of the front is variable according to customer wishes. In this model with its large fenders, the Marchal main headlights are concealed behind plexiglas covers.

250 GT Coupé Pinin Farina

Within the vast range of Ferrari models from the most exotic to the almost mundane, the 250 GT Coupé has a place reserved among the greatest of classics. It was an imposing car whose looks defied its agility. Shown to the press in June 1958, the 250 GT looked less like a derivative of its predecessor, the Boano and Ellena coupé, but more of a counterpoint to it. In comparison the waist line was lower, its windows were taller and it had very pronounced horizontal lines. Before its public launch at the Paris Salon it was secretly entered in a *concours d'élégance* in Antibes, although its cover was quickly blown because of its registration plate, PROVA MO 58.

The 250 GT came from the new Farina factory in Grugliasco and shared its birthplace with the cabriolet and dream cars destined for more modest budgets, such as the Alfa Romeo Giulietta Spider and the Lancia B24.

It was therefore possible to think in terms of a production run with Farina's build capacity, and indeed 343 cars were built, which constituted a record at the time. The car remained unchanged throughout the production run, until some modifications were introduced in 1959: adoption of an electric overdrive made by Laycock de Normanville, telescopic dampers, the 128 DF engine with spark plugs above the exhaust

In June 1958, Ferrari presented a coupé with a simple understatement and a generously glazed pavilion – the 250 GT Pinin Farina. A coupé for the connoisseur.

The Pinin Farina coupé presented itself as the ideal touring vehicle for two people and their luggage. The Ferrari name on the rear and the discreet Pinin-Farina arms on both flanks identify this racy coupé as a steed from the very best of stables.

manifolds and Dunlop disc brakes. These last two changes were indispensable, as even the most accomplished Ferrari owner needed 45 minutes to change the plugs, while the drum brakes left something to be desired, especially when cold.

In September 1960 John Bolster, who was technical editor of the highly respected British magazine *Autosport,* gave an enthusiastic report on a day spent at Goodwood racetrack, where he was given the opportunity to try no less than three Ferraris, placed at his disposal by the importer, Maranello Concessionaires: a road-going Testa Rossa, a Berlinetta SWB as well as a Coupé. This last one was a demonstration

model first registered in 1958 and with 40,000 kilometres (25,000 miles) on the clock. It had been updated with the exception of the overdrive.

Bolster described this great car as being spacious, luxuriously but sensibly appointed and well-finished. Below 6000 rpm the engine could hardly be heard and gear selection was as precise as one could hope for. He heaped praise on the brakes, which were servo-assisted courtesy of Bendix. John Bolster was not in the first flush of youth, but after a few hours of Ferrari driving admitted to feeling younger. Readers could share the same pleasure in exchange for £6,326 2/6d., tax included.

The front with its flat radiator grille lent the coupé a wider appearance than was actually the case.

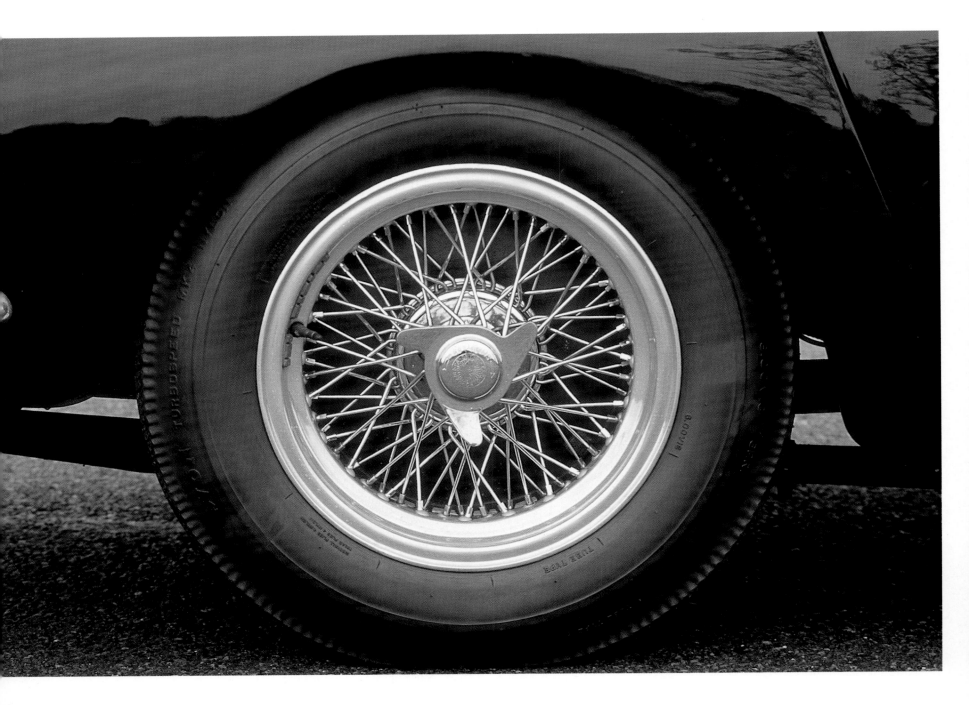

It was naturally also available with right-hand drive for well off customers from the British Isles.

250 GT Berlinetta SWB

This was one of those mechanical creations that made you forget you were simply looking at an inanimate object, feline grace on four wheels and an animal character expressed through the roar of its twelve cylinder engine, whose inlet and exhaust were only barely silenced.

It was the sound and fury of Ferrari. Easy to drive on the road, it had a fearsome reputation on the track; a Jekyll and Hyde in the purest tradition of the Maranello berlinettas, but with a little something extra.

At the peak between ancient and modern times, an intermediate version appeared in June 1959. It still used the existing long chassis, but adopted the shape of the future, with the exception of a small glass area behind the side windows. This had disappeared from the short wheelbase (2400 mm, 7'10") 250 GT shown by Ferrari and Farina at the Paris Salon of October 1959. Suddenly everything was in perfect harmony and the abbreviation of short wheelbase to SWB became the accepted shorthand for a legend in the history of the marque.

In the course of the next few months, five vents appeared, behind the front wheels and above the rear windows, to improve air circulation and the comfort of passengers. Because of its luxury fittings, the Lusso version which developed 240 horsepower weighed approximately 110 kilos (240 lbs) more, while the competition version put out 280 and even 293 horse-power thanks to the adoption of the Testa Rossa engine. Additionally, the doors and bonnet were made of light alloy and in some instances the entire body was made of aluminium.

The potency of the 250 GT Berlinetta SWB can be recognized even when standing still. Under the aluminium hood the three-litre V12 engine with 280 bhp waits nervously for the gas pedal's commands, which it immediately translates into forceful propulsion.

Its list of racing successes is endless and its drivers came from all corners of the globe; the American journalist Denise McCluggage, the French ski champion Henri Oreiller, and the Briton who was a true genius behind the wheel, Stirling Moss. At the wheel of the berlinetta owned by his patron and team chief, Rob Walker, Moss won the 1960 Tourist trophy with the radio on full blast!

Wolfgang Seidel, a racer from Düsseldorf, lent his black version to the German magazine *Motor Revue* on two conditions – one week and no more than 1000 kilometres (620 miles). The writer Heinz-Ulrich Wieselmann, who had honed his racing skills by competing on several occasions in the Mille Miglia, described the car thus: "as sweet as a summer love … the ultimate pleasure on four wheels still available to a select few in the era of mass motoring". To drive a Ferrari was "to drive in silk". With a strong hand and a heavy foot, he measured that it took 22 seconds to accelerate from 0 to 100 mph (160 kph) and brake to a complete standstill. He did not hide the car's needs from his readers: 16 to 18 litres per 100 kilometres (15 to 13 mpg) and a set of Dunlop Racing tyres every 3000 km (1850 miles) if driven hard.

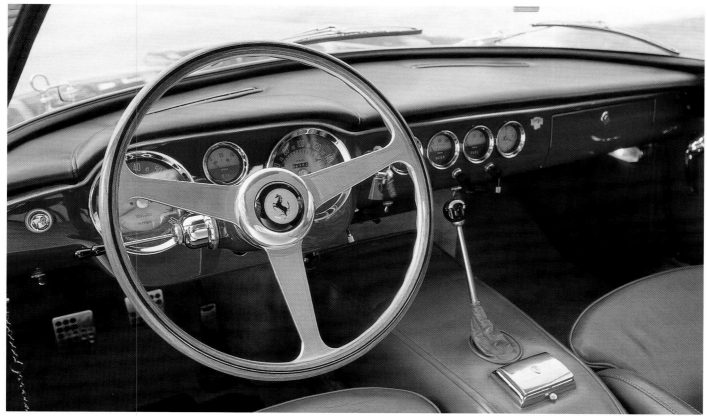

There is hardly a more sensuous rear in the entire automobile world than that of the Berlinetta SWB. It was submissive on the road, and feared on the track – its opponents could at least enjoy its successful rear design.

Behind the Borrani spoke wheels Ferrari installed disk brakes, the hot air could escape through side vents. The Ferrari V12 engine with its powerful sound was a well-known sight.

400 Superamerica

At a time when even Ferraris began to resemble one another, a few wealthy nonconformists exercised their right to own a purely personalized version. And their requests did not fall on deaf ears. The diversification game was played to the full: greater luxury, more power, prestige and individualism expressed around a few constant factors, such as the most recent Colombo engine with exterior spark plugs and 3967 cc. Its horsepower was apparently upped to 400, which would explain the car's model number, although on the test bed it only showed 340. The wheelbase was 2420 mm (7'11"), which in the autumn of 1962 went up to 2600 mm (8'6"), the same as the last 410 SAs. Added to this were Dunlop disc brakes and Koni telescopic dampers and the Laycock de Normanville electric overdrive.

Basically there were 45 variations, as this was the actual number built. The changing of the guard from the preceding model, the 410 SA, was done discreetly, by way of an angular coupé destined for Fiat's future boss, Gianni Agnelli. It had an almost square radiator grille, a panoramic windscreen, a roof with a clear panel and twin headlights. There were also six convertible models with obvious links to the 250 GT Cabriolet.

The Ferrari 400 Superamericas were almost only produced in the Pinin Farina factory. At the critical points in the development of this model stood four coupés which pointed the way forward for the future. The Superfast 2, shown at the Turin show in November 1960, was without a doubt one of the most important cars, in stylistic terms, of its era. It had smooth lines which, when viewed from the side, appeared to take their inspiration from the wing of a plane, even in the design of the lights which were protected behind metal covers.

The simple rear lights of the 400 Superamerica were embedded in massive chrome frames. This took away their elegance and optical clarity.

The Coupé Special Aerodinamico launched at the 1961 Geneva show took practical matters into consideration. Cooling for both the occupants and mechanical parts was assured by an imposing air intake on the bonnet and windows with quarter-lights. The headlights were no longer hidden and the covers for the rear wheels as on the Superfast 2 were only an option. One year later, again at Geneva, the Superfast 3 appeared with slim roof pillars, large glass areas, while the radiator could be blanked off by a thermostatically controlled blind.

However, the Superfast 4 was less attractive, with two pairs of headlights mounted in the end of the wings as dictated by a whim of fashion. Ferrari historians confirm that this car used the same chassis as the model presented in Turin in 1960, but modernised to suit the times. This model was never to shine under the harsh lights of a motor show, unlike the precursor to the final generation of 400 Superamericas displayed in London in October 1962. The additional 180 mm (7") on the wheelbase could be seen in the increase in area between the doors and the line of the rear wheels.

The lines of the 400 Superamerica, nicknamed Aerodinamico, were characterized by flowing forms and a filigree roof construction.

From a time when Ferrari drivers still smoked: the dainty ashtray placed on the leather bound central console, shows a love of detail. Three double Weber carburetors crown the twelve-cylinder engine and its 400 bhp.

250 GTE Coupé 2+2

The 24 Hours of Le Mans race held on 25th and 26th June 1960 was a true Ferrari festival. Its drivers snapped up seven of the top eight places, with victory going to the Belgian duo, Olivier Gendebien and Paul Frère in a TR 60. Always ready to take to the track at the Sarthe circuit, the race director's car also caused a minor sensation. It was a Ferrari 2+2 coupé, built in the utmost secrecy, and nothing had leaked out about this project.

In a daring display, Farina had managed to pull together three very different ingredients. Onto a 2600 mm (8'6") wheelbase he grafted a big twelve cylinder engine in its most modest guise of 240 horsepower, at the same time as building a cabin big enough to accommodate four passengers, without compromising the raciness and class that everyone expects from a Ferrari. The engine was therefore moved forward by 200 mm (8"), and although it had a 55 to 45 percent weight distribution, on the road the 250 GTE tended towards slight understeer. That same year in October at the Paris Salon, the GTE had its world première. It was this first production car that Enzo Ferrari used as personal transport. Fans of this model maintained that the rear seats were remarkably comfortable. Doubtless, it was well proportioned. A great deal of preparation work had been carried out in the wind tunnel. A thin horizontal moulding served to soften the lines of this imposing

The rear lights, brought together as an ensemble in a chrome frame, adorned the elegant rear of the 250 GTE, which had its debut at the Geneva show of March 1963.

Commendatore Enzo Ferrari
preferred using the
250 GTE, with its most
successfully designed form,
for his private journeys.
The horizontal beading lent
the Pinin Farina creation a
welcome lightness of form.

coupé. Apart from the version that ran at Le Mans, which had smooth sides, the first prototypes had side air vents built into the bodywork, while on the production model these were fitted to an additional panel. For the next 30 months production ran at approximately one car per day. An overdrive operated by a lever on the steering column was offered only with the shorter of the two final drive ratios available.

The 250 GTE had no reason to envy the performance, the comfort and the prestige of the grandest of tourers. When a group of American journalists visited Maranello, works driver Phil Hill took the wheel of the Paris show car with two passengers on board. He put it through the wringer which had previously seen off its nearest rival, the Aston Martin DB4,

acceleration from 0 to 100 mph (100 kph) then braking to a standstill in 25 seconds.

Not bad compared to the Berlinetta which could do the same in 22 seconds.

At the 1963 Geneva show, the GTE appeared with some small changes. The fog lights previously fitted at the edges of the radiator grille were now mounted under the main lights, which had a chrome ring as on an earlier version. The rear lights were all grouped together vertically while the rear edge was steeper. The Borrani rims were wider and the rear dampers were combined with helical springs.

In its last phase, about 49 were produced to this specification. This model took the name 330 America and had a four litre engine under the bonnet.

A total of eight instruments informed the driver of the wellbeing of the twelve-cylinder, 240 bhp engine with its three-litre capacity. Enough to provide a top speed of 220 kph (137 mph).

Dino 246 SP
Dino 196 SP
Dino 286 SP
Dino 248 SP
Dino 268 SP

For Enzo Ferrari, the first name Dino had two sides: on the human side, the one was tragic, while on the commercial and sporting side the other was extremely profitable.

Dino was the name of his son, who died of leukaemia in 1956. Dino was also the name of the shrines he built in his honour, cars with six and eight cylinders, including in 1957, the first single-seater, then in 1958 the first sports prototype, and finally in 1967 the first production car.

These cars could be recognized by their code numbers; thus the 156 F2 was a Formula 2 car with a 1.5 litre six cylinder engine. This operation based on nostalgia started in a modest fashion, and it was only from 1961 that the Dino name really prospered. Enzo Ferrari presented the 156 F1 at a press conference in February at the same time as the 246 SP. Their family ties were immediately apparent. The two cars bore the strong signature of Carlo Chiti, who was in charge of the project. Following the technical revolution started by the Englishman John Cooper, the engine was located at the rear.

Chiti was also responsible for the radiator intake in the form of two oval holes, as well as testing in the wind tunnel, the usefulness of which was quickly appreciated at Maranello. The side windows and the rear bodywork went all the way to the rollover bar, and only a removable top was needed to create a Targa look.

According to Richie Ginther who test drove it, no other sports car stuck to its line so easily. The

Scuderia Ferrari started at the European Hillclimb Championship race with the Dino 268 SP. Ludovico Scarfiotti contested the 1962 race in the 268 SP.

Engines with six and eight cylinders were in operation in the Dino models, named after Enzo Ferrari's son who had died of leukaemia. The 268 SP's V8 had a capacity of 2.6 litres.

Dino 246 SP · Dino 196 SP · Dino 286 SP · Dino 248 SP · Dino 268 SP

pronounced rear lip on the car was rather like a spoiler ahead of its day. But it was in fact intended to prevent exhaust gases from getting into the cockpit. It soon proved to have a positive effect on increasing downforce on the rear wheels.

While the Grand Prix cars were much in evidence and dominated the world of Formula 1, the 246 SP performed less brilliantly in the world of sports cars. It had to content itself with one win in the 45th Targa Florio on the 30th April, in the expert hands of Count von Trips and Olivier Gendebien.

It laid the groundwork, however, for the following season. The fiery Ricardo Rodriguez, the equally temperamental Willy Mairesse and the calm Olivier Gendebien won the Targa Florio in a 246 SP, then Gendebien, this time partnered by Phil Hill, took the same car to victory in the Nürburgring 1000 Kilometres.

At the traditional press conference held on 24th February 1962, a whole fleet of Dinos was unveiled. The 196 SP, the 286 SP, as well as the eight cylinder 248 SP were rapidly followed by the 268 SP with the V8 bored out to 2644.9 cc. They were nearly all identical, with a lower rear end and openings behind the doors to improve the brake cooling. But for various reasons the hoped-for success did not materialize, except in the European Hillclimb Championship that Ludovico Scarfiotti won with the agile 196 SP.

250 GTO Series I
250 GTO Series II

Enzo Ferrari triggered the great upheaval and it happened in 1960. The Fédération Internationale de l'Automobile had had enough of Ferrari's supremacy in sports car racing. So for 1962 a new technical regulation was drawn up. The World Championship would be for Grand Tourers, and Jaguar and Aston Martin threatened to come and cause trouble like sharks out at sea.

"What we need", said the Commendatore to his two chief engineers, Giotto Bizzarrini and the boss of Scaglietti, Sergio Scaglietti, "is a car that is small, light and based on the Berlinetta". The two men rolled up their sleeves as never before and never again, and got down to work, while their taskmaster enquired constantly as to the state of progress when he visited them. Bizzarrini set to, stiffening to the maximum the 2400 mm (7'10") wheelbase chassis.

In collaboration with Carlo Chiti, he also undertook the job of improving the engine by using higher profile camshafts, bigger valves and a new exhaust manifold. And in what was surely an incredible sight for the experts, a veritable cathedral of injection sprang from the V of the twelve cylinder engine, in the shape of six double-bodied Weber Type 38 DCNs. Meanwhile, in the Scaglietti workshops in the Via Emilia Est in Modena, the best panel beaters in the business were labouring to model the aluminium panels to fit a design that Enzo Ferrari himself had sketched out.

Beauty was not on the list of imperatives but it came logically as it followed function, even in areas where air flow and heat had to share the same space. Bizzarrini located the engine near the cockpit so

The GTO was the king of the Gran Turismos of the early 1960s. It won three constructor's world championships for the company fron Maranello.

that two (and later three) side vents were needed to extract the air.

The three half-moon shaped openings in the front end, designed to allow the engine to breathe, underlined the look of contained power in the same way as the spoiler lip on the rear of the tail as used in the GTO's first race at Sebring in 1962, and later fully integrated into the design. At the end of 1961, Bizzarrini, Chiti and a few other rebels left Ferrari in a rage.

The project was handed over to the genial and nervous Mauro Forghieri. The bosses changed but the work continued. As was the way of the company, the work progressed in radical fashion after the GTO (the O stood for *omologata*, homologated) was shown by Enzo Ferrari to a respectful audience at his press conference on 24th February 1962. To its credit went three world titles from 1962 to 1964, and drivers such as Graham Hill, Innes Ireland, Mike Parkes, Willy Mairesse and the legendary partnership of Pierre Noblet/Jean Guichet divided up between them the rest of the spoils.

There appeared some strange hybrids, including some models with a modified four litres engine from the Superamerica. In 1964 the second series of GTOs (three new cars and four old ones with new bodywork) appeared less spectacular. But the GTO was the queen of the GTs during the sixties, as Stirling Moss once said. It was the ultimate expression of a front-engined Ferrari, a jewel in the history of the motor car and as timeless as a Botticelli.

Scaglietti in Modena gave the aluminium body its successful shape; a bold spoiler edge at the rear improved the aerodynamic, as did the masked headlights.

Six Weber double carburetors provided the twelve-cylinder engine with an optimal mixture. The driver kept the built-in rev counter constantly in view, for the 300 bhp strong engine produced around 7500 rpm.

The last version of the GTO presented itself with a strongly modified body, which had been more intensely tailored to the requirements of racing sport.

Two plain rear lights
adorn the aerodynamically
optimized rear of the GTO
in its final form. It was
almost unbeatable from
1962 to 1964.

250 GT Lusso

It was called Lusso because of the abbreviation GT/L on its type plate. The name was coined by a circle of admirers of the marque and it became as famous as Tour de France or Daytona. For all that, it was hardly luxurious, with just enough room for two passengers and additional space for luggage behind the bucket seats. To get inside, it was preferable to be young and slim, as the back rests could not be tilted.

Apart from some matt black leather on the dashboard there was hardly any trim. However, its beauty was never in doubt. It had light flowing lines which successfully combined straights and curves, large glass areas with just a slim pillar between the rear side windows and the large rear window. This shape was popular for a long time. In 1975, when a jury was tasked with choosing the sixty most beautiful cars

built since 1903 for an exhibition at the New Harbor Art Museum in California, the Ferrari 250 GT/L took all the votes.

This great lady of the car world could permit itself a late arrival at its debut at the Paris Salon in October 1962, accompanied by Battista Pininfarina. (In 1961, with the agreement of the Italian government, the surname Pinin, which means dwarf in Italian, had

The 250 GT Lusso, once again a Pininfarina design, took the role of automobile ideal beauty of the early 1960s. It had its debut at the Paris Automobile Show of October 1962.

250 GT Lusso

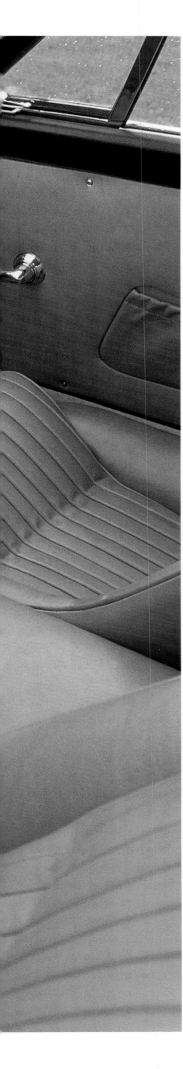

The speedometer and rev counter were placed centrally on the dashboard, which was not well appreciated by all buyers. Leather and wood provided an adequate Ferrari ambience for the interior.

been added to the family name of the master of Grugliasco to form his working name.)

The Lusso could not hide its ancestry. Its links with the SWB Berlinetta were obvious. It had in fact used the same chassis, even if the tubing was of a thinner section and the engine had been moved forward to give the occupants more room. The Watt linkage from the differential casing to the front axle had been lifted from the GTO and the engine characteristics were similar to those of the Berlinetta and the GT 2+2.

The layout of the instruments on the Lusso was somewhat unusual: the speedometer and the rev counter were slightly to the right above the gear lever, angled towards the driver's field of vision. Four dials of secondary importance were situated just behind the Nardi steering wheel, which was mounted almost vertically.

Although this car approached perfection, the journalist Count Giovanni Lurani Cernuschi complained about the lack of a fifth gear. The specialist American publication, *Road & Track,* which had previously tested the Lusso in June 1969 and ranked it as one of the great classics, also noticed the characteristic vibration of the 250 GT engine at 3700 rpm.

This was no longer a complaint after 1964. The 250 GT/L was one of the great tradition of 250 GTs. It provided a full stop to this range, last but certainly not least.

Gliding lines in a harmonious interaction of straights and curves with a lot of glass characterized the beautiful form of this coupé with Borrani spoke wheels.

250 LM

Shown at the Paris Salon in November 1963, the first 250 LMs (LM for Le Mans) actually had a three litre engine. However the 31 other cars built had a 3.3 litre power unit hidden under the bonnet, to the extent that in true Ferrari fashion they should have been called the 275 LM.

The wily Commendatore did not want to jeopardise the new car's homologation into the GT category. The FIA acted in a bureaucratic manner and delayed proceedings, withholding its approval until 19th February 1966. By that time Scaglietti had already ended the production run. The 250 LM designed by Pinin-

farina was the first commercially available mid-engined Ferrari. The windscreen, the side windows and the roof were the same as on the second GTO series. Just behind the grille were the oil and water radiators and the tank for the dry sump lubrication. Boot space was at the front and the spare wheel was

A revolutionary from Maranello: The 250LM was the first Ferrari mid-engine vehicle available for purchase. Ferrari won the 1965 Le Mans 24-hours race with it.

in the back with the driving position moved forward. After trying the car, John Blunsden wrote in *Motor Racing:* "This must have been the type of feeling experienced by drivers of the pre-war Auto Unions."

During a test day at Brands Hatch, Blunsden was lent by John Drummond, for a period of forty minutes, the car he entered in races for the Marquis Rolo Fielding. Cautiously, Blunsden restricted himself to using the first three speeds of the non-synchro five

speed box. They had to be treated carefully and would howl in protest if the engine speed was not perfectly matched.

The competition life of the 250 LM began quietly. A sad fate, however, awaited the car originally displayed in Paris. It was sold to Luigi Chinetti's NART team; retired in its first race, finished eighth in its second outing and was destroyed totally in a fire on its third outing at Sebring.

The 250 LM is reminiscent of the GTO from the front view; otherwise, this Ferrari was conceived without compromise for action on the racetrack. Graham Hill and Jochen Rindt were among the most successful 250 LM drivers.

All the same, by the end of the 1964 season the 250 LM had won ten major events, notably the 12 Hours of Reims on the 5th July with Graham Hill and Jo Bonnier. In 1965, Ferrari's honour in this category was left in the hands of privateers. The greatest win was without a doubt the 24 Hours of Le Mans on 19th and 20th June, scored by the LM of the North American Racing Team in the hands of Jochen Rindt and Masten Gregory who, it is true to say, profited from the many retirements in the race.

Englishman David Piper won numerous events at the wheel of his 250 LM, patriotically painted in British Racing Green. Which no doubt explains why to this day Piper does what he has always loved doing; racing Ferraris, the same ones as in those years.

The mid-mounted twelve-cylinder engine operated with a capacity of 3.3 litres producing 320 bhp. This powerhouse achieved a top speed of 287 kph (178 mph).

330 GT 2+2

Sometimes," Sergio Scaglietti was keen on saying, "when Pininfarina submits a new drawing, we are gripped by a feeling of panic. Will the public accept it? And then a few months later the answer is positive. He has an incredible sense of what is right."

He was, however, also capable of getting it wrong, especially when the wizard of Grugliasco abandoned his philosophy of noble simplicity to follow the whims of a passing fashion. This was the case with the 330 GT 2+2, which Enzo Ferrari showed to a handful of journalists at his press conference on 11th January 1964 before exposing it to the eyes of the world at the Brussels Motor Show a little later. Some onlookers could not believe their eyes as the twin headlights looked like strange protuberances. In August of that year, the journalist Gregor Grant wrote in *Autosport:* "As to the rear, he could have designed something less plain."

The wood veneer did not please him either, as he felt it was but a pale imitation of the interior of British luxury cars. "Apart from that" said Grant, "there are not enough superlatives to describe this Maranello four-seater." Based on the Superamerica, the engine was sublime and the torque of this four litre unit had improved a lot compared to the nervous 250 GTs in their development years. Grant felt the 300 horse-power claimed by the factory was a little on the conservative side, and he could only praise the work of the Ferrari technicians for their work on the 330 GT's exhaust system. The sound was at the same time engulfing, raucous and piercing. The chassis had been stretched by 50 mm (2") to 2650 mm (8'8"), which translated into a 10 cm (4") increase in rear leg room, whereas occupants of the 250 GT 2+2 only

The 330 GT was the first Ferrari to carry double headlights, and those being of different sizes. Not everyone greeted this solution with applause.

had occasional seats, barely big enough to accommodate dwarfs on condition they had no legs. The 330 GT was generally more luxurious, starting with its comfortable Reutter system seats.

Then there was the ride, to which the multitalented Mike Parkes, in charge of research as well as a Ferrari racing driver, had turned all his attention. Although firmer it was not excessively harsh.

For the second generation, Pininfarina had removed many of the items that had drawn complaints. Single headlights now adorned the front, while on the side,

three large openings replaced the previous slits that had been laid out in a 4/3/4 design. Steel wheels replaced the traditional Borrani wire rims, which were only available on demand. Instead of the four speed box with Laycock de Normanville overdrive which switched off automatically when shifting down to third, it offered a new five speed all-synchromesh box which had no effect on the top speed of 245 kph (152 mph).

In any case, this was a purely academic figure in the United States, the car's main export market.

The side view of the 330 GT could persuade even its
strongest critics. With its 2.56-metre (8'5") wheelbase,
it was a well laid out, real 2+2 seater.

Reminiscent of the Zeitgeist were the double headlights; the four-litre engine with 300 bhp indulged its owners with a hefty torque and an exciting melody. Comfortable leather seating provided the travel luxury of the Gran Turismo.

500 Superfast

Some people referred to it as the Ferrari Royale, but unlike the similarly named Bugatti, the 500 Superfast was actually acquired by crowned heads and nobility such as Shah Reza Pahlevi, who was so impressed with it that he bought two, and Prince Bernard of the Netherlands. Some rich celebrities also got caught up in its spell, as was the case with the German playboy Gunther Sachs and the English actor Peter Sellers, and the Greek shipping magnate Niarchos.

The robust model number 500 was a reference this time to the size of the engine. An equally round and impressive figure was attached to the horsepower developed by the five litre unit: 400. It was in the spring of 1964 at the Geneva Motor Show that this model first caught the eye of the general public. The Aerodinamico coupé of 1961 had an obvious influence on its lines, although the rear end stopped more abruptly. With its flat sides and its stretched radiator grille underlined by basically decorative bumpers, as was its rear registration plate, the 500 Superfast gave the impression of being much longer than it really was. The rolling chassis was the same as on the 330 GT, but it had been improved with the addition of more efficient Dunlop discs fitted with a dual circuit and a servo, adjustable Koni dampers, and leaf springs supported by helical springs at the rear.

The cabin had all the atmosphere of a boudoir. The leather for the seats had required the sacrifice of only

The Shah of Iran, Playboy Gunter Sachs, and Prince Bernhard of the Netherlands were among the 37 buyers of a Ferrari 500 Superfast. The side grills ensured a good dispersion of engine room heat.

the most noble of cattle. As for the instruments, they were embedded in the best possible veneer.

From October 1963 to August 1966 37 examples of the Pininfarina masterpiece were produced with the utmost care. The first one was delivered on 23rd October 1964 by the German concessionaire, Auto Becker in Düsseldorf, to the Consul Osterfeld at Wunstorf, and the last was sent to Colonel Ronnie Hoare's Maranello Concessionaires outside London. 29 left-hand drive models were built, the rest being right-hand drive.

25 cars were built in the first run and the 12 others were built after December 1965 in a second batch. They benefited from the improvements already made to the 330 GT 2+2: five speed mechanical gearbox in place of the Laycock de Normanville overdrive, suspended pedals and three large side vents to cool the engine compartment instead of the eleven little slits.

Some cars are worth millions, others are designed for millionaires. Without a doubt the Ferrari 500 Superfast fits into the latter category.

Plane flanks and a long front overhang let the Superfast appear bigger than it actually was. Nevertheless, it remained a vehicle for long distances with comfortable seating and many interior comforts.

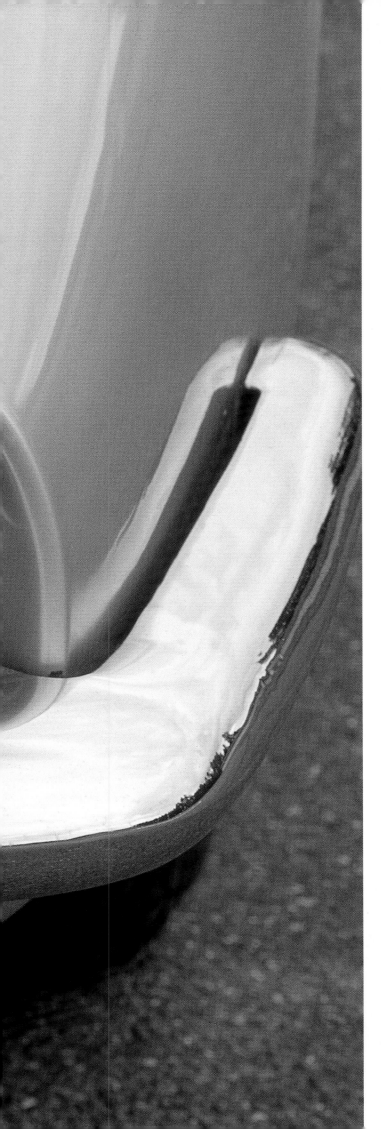

The 500 possessed only small fender corners, both at the front and at the rear, which played more of an alibi role than they provided serious defense in case of a contact situation.

275 GTB
275 GTS
275 GTB/4
Spider NART

It was side by side with its sister car, the 275 GTS (S for Spider) that the Ferrari 275 GTB was revealed at the Grand Palais in Paris in October 1964.

A few little details gave them an air of *déjà-vu*. There were similarities with the first and second series GTO, as well as allusions to the GT/L that it followed. The wheels even resembled those of the 156 F1 of 1963, while the beautiful Borrani wire

wheels were only available as an option. But as usual, with his skill at combining ancient and modern, Pininfarina could not be accused of plagiarism. A long bonnet, a highwaist line and a truncated boot; the shape of the GTB expressed its strengths. The 3.3 litre engine developed 280 horsepower, and in order to improve weight distribution, the differential was attached to the five speed gearbox.

The fact that it boasted independent suspension attested to its racing parentage, a line including the 250 LM. One year later the scene was repeated in the same theatre: the rear window had grown in size, the hinges for the boot had been moved to the outside to increase its capacity. Further modifications appeared when the car was shown at the Brussels show in January 1966.

One of the many successful form details of the 275 GTB: The generous hip curves in the style of a Rubens painting contrast with the graphically striking ventilation slits.

On the outside the radiator grille had been moved forward while the Campagnolo wheels were reminiscent of those on the 1965 P2. Mechanically, a rigid housing enclosed the drive shaft from the engine to the differential-gearbox unit.

Between May and August 1966, twelve 275 GTB/Cs (C for Competition) were built. They had been lightened with plexiglass windows, fitted with wider rims, and the engine, now equipped with a dry sump, had its power increased to 300 horsepower.

This was the same power output as the GTB/4, its successor, shown in Paris in October 1966, although the GTB/4 featured four overhead camshafts rather than two to control the 24 valves.

From the outside it was recognisable by the bulge in its bonnet. The power transmission unit was bolted to the chassis at four points.

The Formula 1 driver Jean-Pierre Beltoise considered it "one of the nicest cars of its era". It was also one of the fastest, and he demonstrated this fact by covering the 75 kilometres (45 miles) from Paris to Nemours at an average speed of 195 kph (121 mph), including the stop at the motorway tollbooth.

Enzo Ferrari would not admit to fathering the NART spider, based on the GTB/4, of which Luigi Chinetti, the dynamic American dealer, had ten built by Scaglietti in Modena. As for the standard GTS, of which 200 were built by Pininfarina himself in Turin between November 1964 and May 1966, they were a touch too soft for American enthusiasts, who had to make do with 260 horsepower and shorter ratios. In the land of opportunity, it was important to have the power, if not the courage to use it.

The 275 GTS with its
260 bhp behaved in a
tamer manner on the road,
playing more the role of the
gentle beau. Exactly 200
examples were produced by
Pininfarina in Turin.

The form of the 275 GTB – long hood, high waistline, short rear – mirrored its power: 280 bhp and 3.3-litre capacity ensures an impressive top speed of 260 kph (162 mph).

Alloy wheels from Formula 1 supplier Campagnolo were fitted to the 275 as standard. Borrani spoke wheels were only available on request.

The Spider NART ordered by the American Ferrari importer Luigi Chinetti from Scaglietti as a batch of ten, presented itself totally independent in its form.

275/330 P
275/330 P2
330 P3
330 P4

The 1965 P2 made use of a configuration that had not been seen since the 335 S of 1957: four overhead camshafts, two per cylinder bank. A foil against a club, it was a delicate construction compared to the simplicity of the cars coming out of Detroit, with their big rocker-driven seven litre V8 engines, and with which the advancing army of Henry Ford appeared menacingly on the horizon.

The quarrel between the two potentates, Ford and Ferrari, led to a rapid evolution of the P models. Some were open-topped, others closed, and intermediate versions like the P2/3 were slipped in between the evolutions.

In their first year, three power units of 3.3, 4 and 4.4 litres caused headaches for the historians. Many technical solutions were borrowed from Formula 1, for example the semi-monocoque structure and the light-alloy wheels discs, designed, just like the shape of the P2, in the wind tunnel. The cars were built by Piero Drogo's Carrozzeria Sports Cars in Modena. The P2 won the World Championship events at Monza, the Nürburgring and Reims as well as the Targa Florio. The P3, the first photos of which were in circulation in January 1966, was shorter, wider, lower and lighter

This tank cap belongs to a Ferrari 330 P, the Ferrari mid-motor racing sports car which won several world championship marque races in 1965.

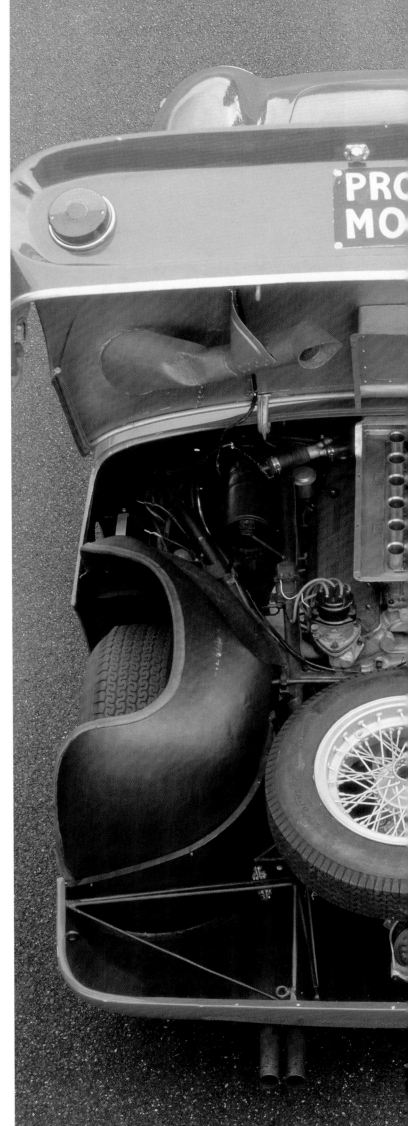

than the preceding model. The spider looked like a Berlinetta with the roof cut off.

As for the chassis, fibreglass had made its appearance. The huge bank of six Weber carburettors had been ripped out and replaced with Lucas fuel injection, which increased the horsepower by ten, to 420. John Surtees and Mike Parkes were triumphant at Monza, Parkes and Ludovico Scarfiotti won at Spa, in cars shod with the Firestone tyres that were to be Ferrari standard in 1967. The 24 Hours of Le Mans on 18th and 19th June was marked by a row between John Surtees and Ferrari's race director, Eugenio Dragoni. The split was announced on the eve of the race. The race ended in disaster as all the factory and semi-works cars were forced to retire while Fords took the first three places.

It was in his enemy's own kingdom that the Commendatore would wipe out this humiliation at the first event of the 1967 season, the Daytona 24 Hours. In a carefully stagemanaged finale, the

The rules of long distance racing demand that the basic fittings include a ready for use reserve wheel. Talking of racing: whether the 275 P from 1963 (above) or the 330 P from 1964 (below and to the side) – the range was granted particularly many important victories and remained in action for a remarkably long period.

275/330 P · 275/330 P2 · 330 P3 · 330 P4

Ferraris which held the first three places crossed the line side by side. There were two 330 P4s and one P3, with all the latest modifications. The 450 horsepower engines had been fine-tuned by the engineer Franco Rocchi. They had thirty-six valves, double ignition and direct injection into the inlet manifolds. The P4s once again dominated Monza and they finally gave Ferrari the World Championship. However, at Le Mans the victory laurels fell yet again to Ford, even if only just. Many years later, Mike Parkes reflected that he had never driven a car so hard for so long.

In the 330 P4 a mechanical Lucas multipoint injection provided the twelve cylinders with fuel in what was an innovation for Ferrari. The performance: 450 bhp.

This 330 P4 from 1967 was the last version of the sport prototype with a four-litre engine. Ferrari beat Ford in the battle for the world championship with this vehicle, including a victory at Daytona.

330 GTC
330 GTS
365 GTC
365 GTS

Trying to find a comparison for the qualities of the 330 GTS, a road tester whose name history has mislaid, writing for the American magazine *Road & Track,* could do no better than to quote a well-loved phrase of Teddy Roosevelt's: "Speak softly but always carry a big stick".

In fact, at the time, this presidential piece of advice could be applied to the entire Ferrari range of road cars, which combined impressive power with relative comfort that bordered on the luxurious. It applied also to the 330 GTC which was prominently displayed at the 1966 Geneva show, between the 275 GTB and the 330 GT 2+2.

Once again, well-known ingredients had been brought together. There were obvious touches of Pininfarina's 500 Superfast at the front and the 275 GTS at the rear; the whole thing topped off with a roof that rested on large glass areas that created good visibility while adding to its look. The chassis was a 2400 mm (7'10") short wheelbase one with independent suspension, and the engine had been slightly modified from the 330 GT 2+2, and was now linked to the gearbox and rear axle unit by a massive housing which contained the prop shaft. Four mounting points were sufficient to attach the whole group to the chassis. Thanks to a great deal of work in this area, the

The open 330 GTS flattered its pilots not only with its delicate elegance, but also with its performance (320 bhp) and dazzling road holding.

cabin was exceptionally quiet. This fact had been spotted by Paul Frère in 1966, writing in the German publication *auto motor und sport,* although it is true that the Belgian, thanks to his experiences as a racing driver, was used to noisier machines.

The car was fitted with comfortable leather trimmed seats, electric windows and a heated rear screen, and air conditioning was an option. Added to this equipment level were irreproachable road-holding and performance. Paul Frère was pleased to reveal that the 330 GTC reacted to movements of the steering wheel like a racing car and only displayed a very

slight understeer when pushed to the limit. The 365 GTC appeared at the Paris Salon in 1968 with an engine that had gained 400 cc and 20 horsepower. Torque had also been improved although maximum speed was unaffected. The only visible difference was the positioning of the air intakes on the bonnet rather than on the flanks. They were situated near the windscreen, whereas previously they had been on the sides just behind the front wheels.

After a short wait, the 330 GTS appeared al the Paris Salon in 1966. It reprised the shape of the 275 GTS, apart from a longer frontal area which it

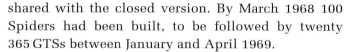

No less than eight instruments informed as to the speed and wellbeing of the engine, while the optional air conditioning of the 330 GTC ensured a cool head.

shared with the closed version. By March 1968 100 Spiders had been built, to be followed by twenty 365 GTSs between January and April 1969.

But a wind of change had got up in the United States and it was heading towards the men from Maranello. Antipollution and safety regulations were making life harder for the fast and beautiful Italian cars.

In spite of this, however, the 330 GTS appeared to lose none of its charm for the American customer, and that cunning, ingenious and still unknown road tester encouraged the reader to buy one.

The 365 GTS inspired
with its clearly designed
rear. Company designer
Sergio Pininfarina once
again set a masterpiece
on Borrani wheels.

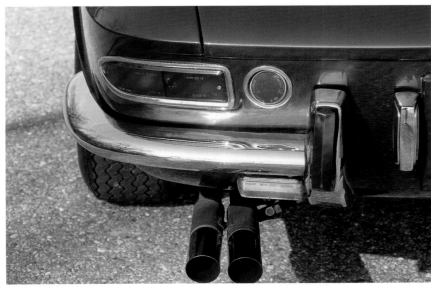

330 GTC · 330 GTS · 365 GTC · 365 GTS

The delicate appearance of the greenhouse with its large amount of glass lends the coupé an optical lightness carried into the interior by the simple Nardi wooden steering wheel.

365 California

Oscar Wilde said he could resist anything except temptation. So one could imagine that, just like visitors to the Geneva show in March 1966, he would have shuddered with pleasure at the sight of the Ferrari 365 California.

Apart from its name and the fact it was a cabriolet, it had nothing in common with the 250 California

Spyder, production of which had ceased three years earlier.

In fact, in spirit it was more of a successor to the 500 Superfast, with a high class power unit and a price to match. In Germany at the time, this noble coupé cost DM 76,000, while price for the three versions of the 330 GT was DM 52,950.

So that its links with the Superfast could never be in doubt, Pininfarina did not hesitate in borrowing certain elements, such as the long curved bonnet set between wings which housed the head-lamps behind plexiglass protectors. Two further retractable lights were fitted above the radiator grille. As was the case with the 1965 Dino 206, the door handles were

Only 14 examples of the luxurious 365 California, available only as a cabriolet, were produced between 1966 und 1967 in the Pininfarina works at Grugliasco near Turin.

combined with the side air intakes. As for the rear, it seemed enormously long and ended in a vertical drop of almost bizarre geometry.

Power steering and Borrani rims were standard. The 4390 cc engine put out 320 horsepower and came from the P2 competition vehicle used in the 1965 season. It was linked to a five speed box, and was fitted in a chassis with a 2650 mm (8'8") wheelbase, which freed up enough room to allow two occasional seats in the rear.

In eighteen months, up to July 1967, fourteen California cabriolets were built in Grugliasco at 78–80 Via Lesna, each one taking almost nine months to build. It was a requiem of sorts for a tradition that Pininfarina had in some way saved from extinction. His achievement could not have been more spectacular.

Characteristic for the 365 California was the noble interior as well as the trapezoidal rear light unit consisting of three round individual lights and the crescent-shaped indicator.

The sonorous appendix was designed to attract well-situated customers from across the Atlantic. After all, in Germany the cabriolet was priced at a proud DM 76,000 in 1967.

Dino 206 S

Small, light, fast – that is how the Dino 206 S can best be characterized. This beautifully shaped racing car performed convincingly on those courses rich in curves such as Targa Florio or the Nürburgring.

The Dino 206 S was made to measure to win the Targa Florio and the events at the Nürburgring, wrote Pete Coltrin in May 1966 in the specialist American magazine, *Road & Track.* The feature was illustrated with photos which showed the car in typical surroundings; alongside a P3 which it resembled as closely as the tiniest Russian doll resembles a big one.

The Dino immediately showed its potential in prototype form as the 166 P. On 23rd May 1965 at the ADAC 1000 Kilometres at the Nürburgring, it had held down third place for a long time in the hands of Lorenzo Bandini and Nino Vaccarella, before eventually finishing fourth. There were murmured complaints that it was a thinly disguised Grand Prix car,

and there were even doubts raised about its claimed cubic capacity of 1.6 litres. Eugenio Dragoni handled these complaints calmly: under official control he dismantled the engine, which was based on a 1961 V6 Formula 1 engine, and the exact capacity of 1593 cc was verified.

Compact, light and easy to handle, these were the basic virtues of the 166 P. It wore the Dino badge to show that it was made by a company affiliated to Ferrari, bearing this name. The project was born as part of a strategy against Porsche. While the German constructor dreamt of outright wins, Enzo Ferrari wanted to be a killjoy in the domain of the Stuttgart constructor, namely the two litre class.

He struck an opening blow by winning the European Hillclimb Championship of 1965. In the fourth round at Cesana-Sestrière Ludovico Scarfiotti was already driving the open 206 P, a car that was powered along by the compact 1987 cc V6 perfected by Franco Rocchi. It was a watered-down version of this engine that was fitted in the 1966 Fiat Dino, and later in the 1967 Ferrari Dino 206 GT.

The 1966 206 S was based on the hillclimb spider. Although similar in appearance, it saved 50 kilos (110 lbs) thanks to a light alloy body resting on a tubular cradle with a fibreglass belly-pan. The plan was to build fifty so that the CSI would homologate it as a sports car. But after sixteen had been built,

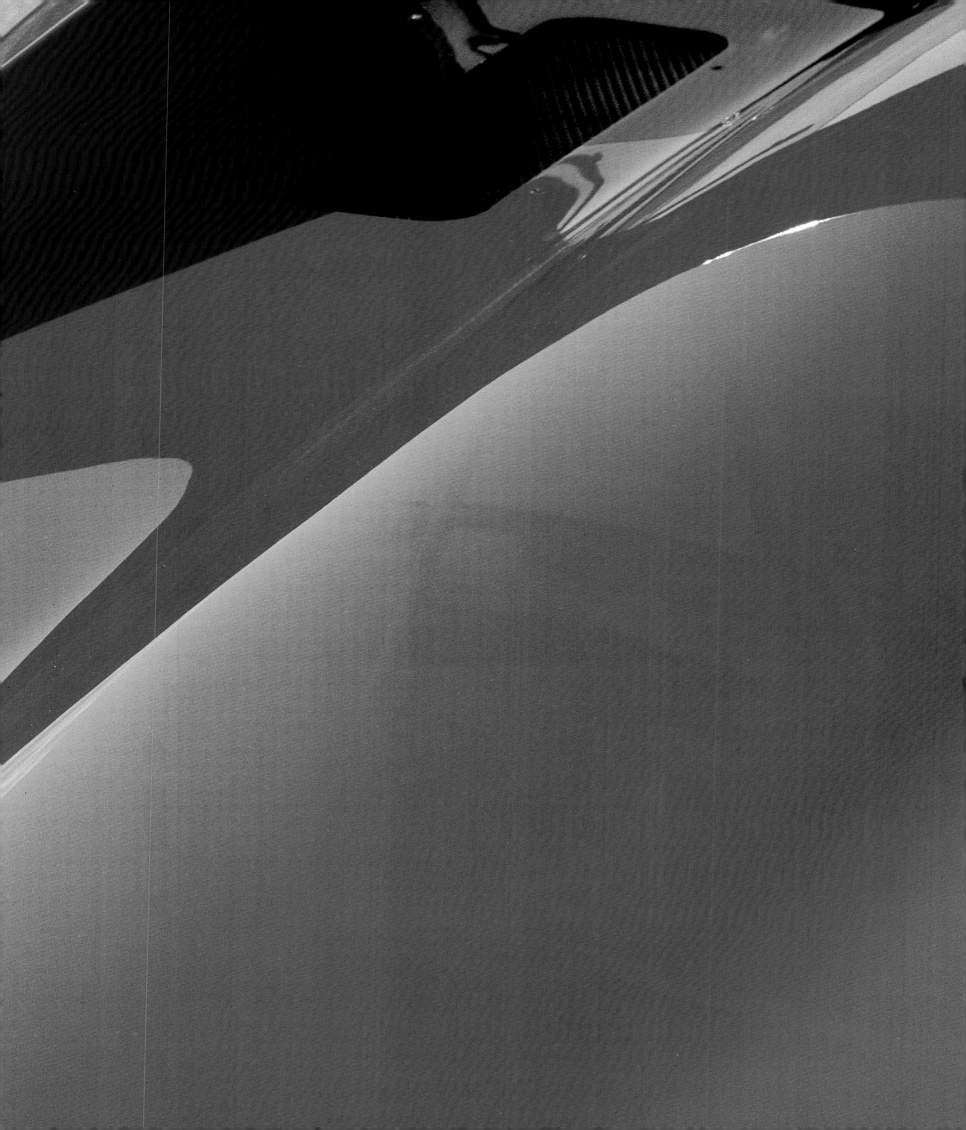

three of them closed, the Carrozzeria Sports Cars at Modena discontinued production, and the Dino had to race as a prototype. It served as a test bed for all sorts of technical experiments such as injection and double ignition as well as two or three valves per cylinder.

On 8th May on the Madonia road circuit that snakes across Sicily, the Dino's race was spoilt by inefficient windscreen wipers, and Jean Guichet and Giancarlo Baghetti finished second. On 5th June in similar conditions, this time at the Nürburgring, Scarfiotti and Bandini finished second again behind the winning Chaparall 2D of Phil Hill and Joakim Bonnier, whose pace they could match when the Swede was at the wheel. The Dino 206 S scored not only with its results but also with its looks.

A compact V-six-cylinder engine powered the Dino, named after Enzo Ferrari's young dead son. The 206 engine only had a capacity of 1.6 litres.

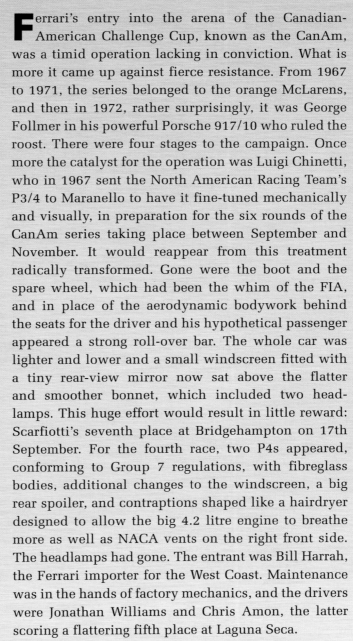

350 CanAm
612 CanAm
712 CanAm

Ferrari's entry into the arena of the Canadian-American Challenge Cup, known as the CanAm, was a timid operation lacking in conviction. What is more it came up against fierce resistance. From 1967 to 1971, the series belonged to the orange McLarens, and then in 1972, rather surprisingly, it was George Follmer in his powerful Porsche 917/10 who ruled the roost. There were four stages to the campaign. Once more the catalyst for the operation was Luigi Chinetti, who in 1967 sent the North American Racing Team's P3/4 to Maranello to have it fine-tuned mechanically and visually, in preparation for the six rounds of the CanAm series taking place between September and November. It would reappear from this treatment radically transformed. Gone were the boot and the spare wheel, which had been the whim of the FIA, and in place of the aerodynamic bodywork behind the seats for the driver and his hypothetical passenger appeared a strong roll-over bar. The whole car was lighter and lower and a small windscreen fitted with a tiny rear-view mirror now sat above the flatter and smoother bonnet, which included two head-lamps. This huge effort would result in little reward: Scarfiotti's seventh place at Bridgehampton on 17th September. For the fourth race, two P4s appeared, conforming to Group 7 regulations, with fibreglass bodies, additional changes to the windscreen, a big rear spoiler, and contraptions shaped like a hairdryer designed to allow the big 4.2 litre engine to breathe more as well as NACA vents on the right front side. The headlamps had gone. The entrant was Bill Harrah, the Ferrari importer for the West Coast. Maintenance was in the hands of factory mechanics, and the drivers were Jonathan Williams and Chris Amon, the latter scoring a flattering fifth place at Laguna Seca.

Ferrari's pitiful lack of competitivity could only be compensated for by increasing engine size. Therefore, for the following season, Mauro Forghieri produced a 6 litre version. Nevertheless, this did not appear

This not especially elegant mirror fastening adorned the Ferrari 712 CanAm, which took part in the American sports car series Canadian-American Challenge Cup, or CanAm for short.

until the final race at Las Vegas on 10th November. It was a rare technical delight with 6222 cc, 48 valves and 620 horsepower. The bodywork had a gigantic wing and aerodynamic brakes controlled by a complex hydraulic system. However, with an all-up weight of 770 kilos (1700 lbs) it was much too heavy. It was the only race in 1968 for a Ferrari sports car, and it ended on a bad note with Chris Amon retiring at the first corner on the first lap.

The next year, the New Zealander was again in the running with a new 612 which was shorter and lighter. The complicated rear wing had been dropped.

Its best result was to be a second place at Edmonton on 27th July. Even a new longer stroke 6.9 litre engine which appeared for the penultimate race was not enough to render it competitive, which only exacerbated an already gloomy situation for Chris Amon, who in any case appeared to suffer from permanent bad luck.

The results were no better when the last rounds were fired in 1971 and 1972: two fourth places for Mario Andretti and Jean-Pierre Jarier. The CanAm Ferraris emitted a raucous but melodious sound, but above all they made a lot of noise about nothing.

The 6.2-litre engine with its 620 bhp was the source of vehement acceleration, while the while the workplace of the driver was spartanly furnished. A four-point safety belt secured the pilot.

Tread pressure on the rear axle could be varied by the adjustable rear spoiler. Powerful Firestone slicks provided the ground contact.

365 GT 2+2

It was often said in the sixties that a Ferrari was an indulgence for two. All the same, at this time fifty per cent of production was of 2+2 versions, although it is true they only vaguely matched the criteria of a four-seater. In such a car, two people could travel like royalty, but if they were four they would get more and more uncomfortable, said Karl Ludvigsen ironically in the December 1968 edition of *Modern Motors*. His remarks could already be applied to the 365 GT 2+2 which, following a well-established tradition, was unveiled at the Paris Salon in October 1967. It was the first Ferrari four-seater with independent suspension, with drilled wheels, the latter being replaced later with five spoke rims like those fitted on the Daytona.

Yet again Pininfarina had sought inspiration from the 500 Superfast, adapting it to the style of the times. The bonnet was long and raked for improved aerodynamics, and the rear was also long and gently sloping until it was abruptly cut off to improve air flow.

This subtle form of self-praise was not to everyone's liking. In January 1968, *Car* wrote that the 365 GT 2+2 was a hotchpotch of different elements dear to Pininfarina's heart. But the generally enthusiastic tone of the piece was already evident from its headline: the most civilised Ferrari ever. And with a dash of patriotic pride, the magazine pointed out that the car had a touch of Britishness about it, as the beautiful savages from Maranello had been developed by Mike Parkes, racing driver and research engineer.

The coupé, whose overall length was almost five metres (16'5"), had good manners that began with a smooth power delivery. The 4.4 litre engine was coupled to the five speed gearbox and linked to the rear axle by an enclosed prop shaft. The whole was fixed to the chassis with two thick silent-blocks at the front and two at the rear. A pneumatic system kept the car level, irrespective of the load. Steel-belted Michelins had replaced the Firestones, which tended

The 365 GT 2+2 was yet another classical Gran Turismo: fast and refined with plenty of room for two passengers and their baggage. The Ferrari fascination could also be enjoyed on short distances by four passengers, albeit in somewhat cramped conditions.

to wear out quickly. They gave the 365 GT 2+2 a contact with the road that could be felt and also heard.
Even the quarter-lights were controlled by humming
electric motors. The front seats were deep and
comfortable, and would move back far enough to
accommodate the tallest of passengers. A foot rest had
been included alongside the clutch pedal.

Driving had been made easy thanks to power-
assisted steering that really constituted a palace coup.
It also upset the purists, as did the air conditioning,
which took up space under the bonnet and added
approximately fifty kilos to the weight.

The 365 GT 2+2 was a heavy car. With a full tank
of fuel it tipped the scales at 1825 kilos (4025 lbs);

considerably more than its mundane rivals like the Chevrolet Camaro and the Ford Mustang.

In this Ferrari, wrote Ludvigsen, performance was not a matter for discussion, nor a cause of arguments, as even the most sensitive wife or girlfriend did not know or cared not at what speed they were travelling.

The 365 GT 2+2 was a heavy car, but was considered, however, as the most refined Ferrari to date at its debut in October 1967.

Dino 206 GT
Dino 246 GT
Dino 246 GTS

The idea of a Ferrari for the people was not in itself a new one. But in attempting to turn the idea into reality one entered into a radical antithesis. In 1960 an 850 cc Ferrarina, known within the company as the "machine gun", had been developed; a slim antithesis to the majestic twelve cylinder cars that bore the Commendatore's name. In 1962 the project was taken up by the industrialist Oronzio De Nova, who dropped it in 1967, having previously set up a company to run it, called ASA (Autocostruzioni Società per Azioni.) The next stage was drawn up in three steps: the styling exercise that was the 206 GT Speciale, shown at the 1965 Paris Salon; the Dino Berlinetta GT glimpsed at Turin in 1966; and finally the Dino 206 GT, also shown at Turin in November 1967. It was already nearly identical to the production car that Scaglietti would build a while later.

Its 1987 cc engine was the fruit of a collaboration with Fiat. It was the Turin manufacturer who delivered the components to Ferrari, where they were assembled after undergoing a few modifications which upped their power by 20 horsepower to 180. Very compact, Franco Rocchi's V6 was joined to a five speed box and differential to form a single unit, with separate compartments to lubricate each component. The unit was transversally mounted, ahead

One of the most beautiful of Ferraris hides behind the simple notation Dino GT, although it was never to bear the glorious name – it possessed only six cylinders.

of the rear axle, allowing for 300 litres (10½ cu.ft.) of boot space behind the engine. The front compartment was taken up entirely by the spare wheel. Scaglietti re-bodied the Dino in aluminium, removed the plexiglass covers over the headlights and added quarterlights to the front side windows. The Dino 206 GT displayed a lovely temperament, and in Sergio Pininfarina's own car Paul Frère clocked 225 kph (140 mph).

After a run of 152 were built, its future was assured when the 246 GT was shown at the 1969 Geneva show. By increasing both the bore and stroke its capacity was raised to 2.4 litres. But it weighed an extra 150 kilos (330 lbs), basically because its engine was made of cast iron rather than siluminum. It produced an extra 15 horsepower and the wheelbase had been increased from 2280 mm (7'6") to 2340 mm (7'8"), as on the pre-production models.

Perfect Pininfarina elegance in blue and red: With the 246 GTS, a Spider version with detachable roof appeared in 1967 alongside the closed coupé.

It could be recognised by its fuel filler, which was now positioned under a flap on the left side of the car, just behind the rear side window. From 1970 onwards, to general disapproval, the Rudge wheels were replaced by five stud fixing wheels. It was at the 1972 Geneva show that the GTS, a version with a removable roof fitted forward of a roll-over hoop but without the triangular side windows, made its first appearance. 1274 examples of this model were built.

The Dinos exported to the United States developed approximately 20 horsepower less and weighed 25 kilos (55 lbs) more, thanks to the antipollution and safety regulations.

It looked like a Ferrari and undoubtedly sounded like a Ferrari. Nevertheless it was never allowed to be called a Ferrari. However, twenty years later, Sergio Pininfarina counted it among his most attractive designs.

The seating position behind the rather low steering wheel took some getting used to. However, the mid-engine two-seater compensated for this with exceedingly agile handling.

365 GTB/4 Daytona
365 GTS/4 Daytona

It was the supreme incarnation of the front engined, rear-wheel drive car. It reached the point where the idea of the motor car escaped its purpose, namely to transport passengers.

The part of the car which contained the engine extended for almost half its total length, followed by a short cockpit and a minimal boot. The gear-change, the steering, the clutch and the brakes all required great strength to operate. As for the air conditioning, it would tend to freeze the limbs closest to it, and would blow little clouds onto the windscreen. It was only after a long apprenticeship that an owner would have a vague idea as to where the bonnet ended, a useful thing to know given the fragile construction of the bumpers, which were essentially there for reasons of style. Once these facts had been accepted, one might find oneself in an overheated cabin, complete with 352 galloping horses. A drive from Heathrow Airport to the Dorchester Hotel in London, and later being stuck in traffic jams to Croydon at five o'clock in the afternoon, is etched in the author's memory.

For this was exactly the type of situation for which the 365 GTB/4 was not designed. It was called Daytona in memory of Ferrari's triple success in this classic American 24 hour event, built for freedom and adventure. It was shown centre stage at the 1968 Paris Salon, at a time of great change. Some of its competitors, like the Lamborghini Miura and the De Tomaso Mangusta had already opted for the centrally mounted engine. With the Ghibli, Maserati still continued with the classic configuration as did Aston Martin. The fastest and best Grand Tourer in the world did not necessarily have to be the most exotic, wrote Dean Batchelor, however, in a sub-heading in the October 1970 edition of *Road & Track*.

While the headlights of the Ferrari 365 GTB were still hidden behind plexiglas at its debut in the fall of 1968, later versions had profane pop-up headlights.

In fact, overall, the Daytona was the best of the bunch, even when it came to top speed. It could hit 275 kph compared to 273 for the Miura, 257 for the Ghibli, 242 for the Mangusta and 238 for the Aston Martin (171 mph to 170, 160, 150 and 148).

It was therefore not surprising that some importers like Charles Pozzi in France and Ronnie Hoare in England, as well as some private buyers, entered the Daytona in competition. At first it was only the privateers, but soon it gained the semi-official back-up of the customer support department at Viale Trento et Trieste in Modena.

Designed by Pininfarina, it was also built in Modena by Scaglietti. From 1971 the band of perspex that formed a belt around the front of the car and enclosed the lights was replaced by retractable headlights, mainly to conform to North American regulations.

The range was increased at the 1969 Frankfurt show with the appearance of the Daytona Spider, mounted on Borrani wire wheels. It was a beautiful and virile car. Only 124 were built, making it a rarity, so that much later, some GTBs were converted to spiders by local craftsmen. Authentic or false – usually one quick glance is all that is required to spot the difference.

The powerful twelve-cylinder engine with its 4.4-litre capacity was capable of 350 bhp, enough for a top speed of 275 kph (171 mph). The in its form beguiling cabriolet is one of today's most converted Ferrari models.

Only 124 examples of the cabriolet named Spider were built. That is why they are so expensive today.

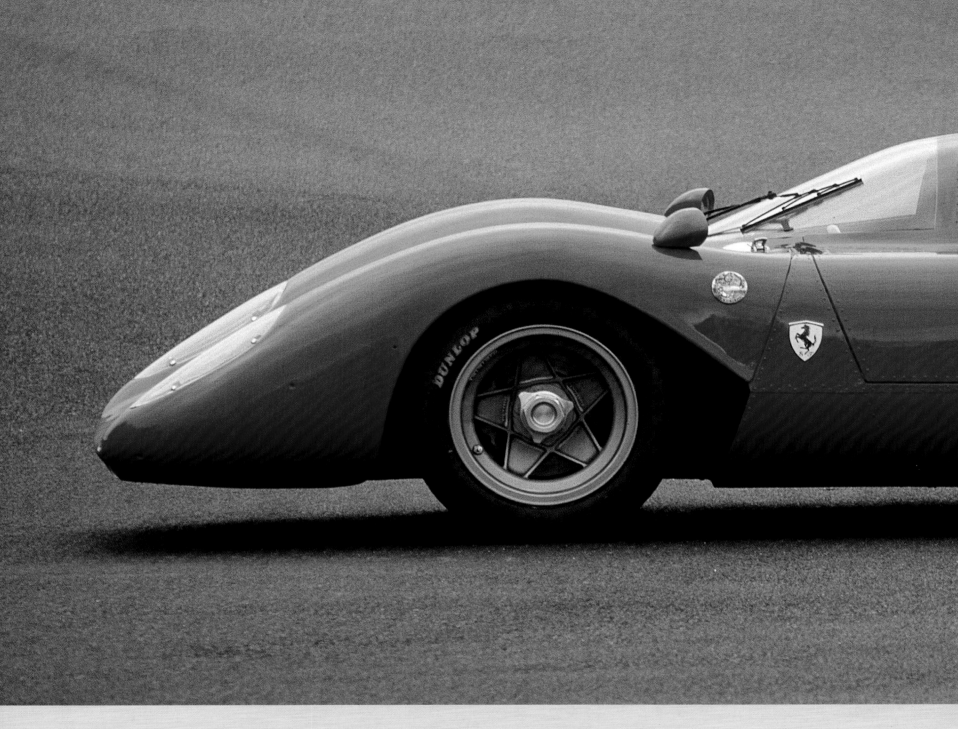

312 P

The 312 P which Ferrari unveiled in mid-December 1968 seemed built to win. Its engine came from the Formula 1 car and had increased in reliability and power since its first appearance, at Syracuse in 1966. At the time of the Italian Grand Prix at Monza in 1966, it had a head with three valves per cylinder. The following year, also at Monza, it had evolved into a 48 valve engine.

In the 312 P this engine developed 420 horsepower, 10 horsepower more than in the 312 F1 Grand Prix single-seater of 1968, as this car had an extremely tortuous exhaust system that presumably robbed it of some power. On the sports car the engine was fitted with Lucas fuel injection and the exhaust gases came out of the side.

The 312 P could easily be mistaken for a smaller version of the 612 CanAm, with the difference that it had headlights, and that the complicated wing system had been done away with. More freedom in the regulations drawn up by the CSI, in the areas of height and the boot, allowed for much cleaner and more functional lines. And it was hoped that the downforce obtained with artificial aerodynamic aids could be compensated for with a radical wedge shape.

The 312 P was the work of a very competent team. Giacomo Caliri was responsible for aerodynamics, Franco Rocchi had developed the engine, Gianni Marelli was in charge of development, and the whole project was overseen by Mauro Forghieri, whose place at the track was taken by Stefano Jacoponi.

The overall results were not satisfying. In six races the 312 P twice finished second, starting with its debut on 22nd March 1969 at Sebring in the hands of Chris Amon and Mario Andretti, and 11th May in the Spa 1000 Kilometres where Pedro Rodriguez and David Piper drove the only spider to be entered. On

Ferrari started at the Le Mans 24 hour race with the closed 312 P Berlinetta, but had to accept defeat at the hands of the Porsche 917.

13th April, in the BOAC 500 run at Brands Hatch, Amon and Rodriguez finished fourth.

At Le Mans, on 14th and 15th June, the two open-top 312 Ps were transformed into Berlinettas with a very long roof. Amon retired on the very first lap after running over debris from John Woolfe's accident in a Porsche 917. The second car, for Pedro Rodriguez/David Piper, retired in the 13th hour. All the same the 312 P was often on pole position, a place it also occupied in the hearts of the public.

There were three reasons for it not fulfilling its promise. Ferrari's efforts were spread too wide: Formula 1, Sports Cars and CanAm. On top of this the Commendatore was already working on the 512 S which was to be the ultimate weapon in the fight against the Porsche 917. With the 908 in the hands of the strong partnership of Joseph Siffert and Brian Redman, the Stuttgart firm lined up as a strong opponent in an area, the three litre class, where the Maranello machines had long ruled the roost. Finally, the only two Ferraris were lined up against a swarm of well-equipped Porsches and Fords, already overcome by sheer numbers.

The engine of the 312 P operated with a capacity of three litres and achieved 420 bhp. Based on the successful twelve-cylinder Ferrari Formula 1 racing cars, it already possessed four valves per cylinder.

512 S
512 M

The 512 S, later the 512 M (for *modificata*) was only a stop-gap between the three litre 312 P and 312 PB. They were brutal cars, violent and noisy, but in one word they were beautiful. Under their lightweight body lurked mechanical components reminiscent of the 612 CanAm and the 312 P; a tubular chassis with bodywork by Cigarla & Bertinetti of Turin glued and riveted to it, a five speed gearbox with limited slip differential, water radiators on each side of the engine, and a centrally mounted oil cooler. Also centrally mounted was a 4994 cc engine with Lucas injection that initially pumped out 550 horsepower.

25 cars were built so that the 512 S could be homologated into Group 5. This was done by January 1970, when it was launched with less ceremony than its main rival Porsche, who had lined up all its cars in the courtyard at Zuffenhausen, like soldiers on parade. Very few of the Berlinettas and Spiders found their way into customers' hands. Most stayed under guard at the factory, while others were to go up in flame and smoke.

The Ferrari 512's futile crusade began at the Daytona 24 Hours on 31st January and 1st February 1970. The Gulf Porsches took first and second place with

Rodriguez/Kinnunen and Siffert/Redman. Third place went to the Ferrari trio of Mario Andretti, Arturo Merzario and Jacky Ickx.

When Mario Andretti, assisted by Nino Vaccarella and Ignazio Giunti, won the Sebring 12 Hours on 21st March, it only served to raise false hopes. The 512 S just emphasised the superiority of the Porsche 917, particularly the Gulf team, run with military precision by men of the calibre of John Wyer and David Yorke.

In the Targa Florio and at the Nürburgring the 512s even had to play second fiddle to the agile Porsche 908/3. The trip to Le Mans on 13th and 14th June was a real disaster. 14 Ferraris were entered, 8 long-tailed versions, and half were works entries. Four were wiped out in one go during the night, when Sweden's Reine Wisell slowed down because of lack of visibility, causing a huge accident for the cars following him.

The 512 M appeared just in time for the last round of the Championship on the 11th October at the Austrian Zeltweg circuit. It weighed 40 kilos (88 lbs) less and developed an extra 70 horsepower. It had a more aerodynamic shape, with small adjustable

Scuderia Ferrari played its part in the Marque championship for sports cars, popular at the time, with the 512 M (for modificata). 25 examples had to be built in order to satisfy the rules.

spoilers and a raised air intake at the rear. At the start, Ickx roared into the lead, but he was forced to retire with electrical problems.

1971 was even worse: eight wins for Porsche, three for Alfa Romeo, but none for the 512 M, not even for the beautifully prepared Roger Penske example, driven by Mark Donohue. On 11th July in the Interserie race at the Norisring, with tragic irony, Pedro Rodriguez was killed driving the 512 M owned by the Swiss Herbert Müller. While the little Mexican had been driving Porsches he had always kept the Ferrari drivers at bay.

Racing cars in the 1970s also had a conventional five-speed manual gear change, with a wooden gearlever knob in the case of Ferrari.

Tread pressure on the rear axle could be varied by the adjustable rear spoiler. Wide slicks provided the frictional connection between the 620 bhp and the track.

312 PB

Small, light, and successful – that was the 312 PB, with which Ferrari dominated sports car racing in 1972. The 312 PB won ten out of eleven races. The Ferrari Formula 1 drivers Jacky Ickx and Clay Regazzoni were the most successful driver duo.

The origins of the Ferrari Boxers, which were in fact V configuration engines with an extremely wide 180 degree angle, go back to the 512 F1 of 1964. This car ran in the last two Grands Prix of the season, at Watkins Glen and in Mexico, helping John Surtees to win the world title. The engine should have been called the 1512, indicating 1.5 litres and 12 cylinders, but the 1 would not fit as Ferrari model numbers would only allow for three figures. The next stage was a two litre unit installed in the graceful 212 E spider, with which, in 1969, the Swiss driver Peter Schetty raced to the top of the European Hillclimbs quicker than all his opponents. Finally the third stage, and provisionally the last: the Formula 1 engine from the 1970 312 B.

This was the unit inherited by the PB, even if, for reasons of reliability needed for endurance racing, horsepower had been reduced by 20, so that it gave about 440. The transmission and suspension also took their inspiration from the single-seater. Following the

example of the Porsche 908/3, it was a small car, the bodywork barely stretching beyond the 2200 mm (7'3") wheelbase. And of course it was also light: 585 kilos (1290 lbs). Rims with simple holes had been used in place of the five spoke wheels, while the headlamps and the two vertical fins located above the rear axle did not appear until later. In 1971 two spiders were built. One was destroyed in its first race at Buenos Aires on 10th January; Ignazio Giunti died in the inferno. The second car, driven by Jacky Ickx and Clay Regazzoni, also had its fair share of accidents, including ones at Monza, Spa and Zeltweg. It actually got to the finish line only once, finishing second on 4th April at Brands Hatch. This meant that its victory in the Kyalami 9 Hours race, a non-championship event, was rather like scoring a goal in football after the final whistle has blown. The 1972 version of the 312 PB had five more horsepower, had become more compact, had been lowered by 50 mm (2") and stood on low-profile

Firestone radial tyres. At the same time, thanks to the use of a heavier tubular structure, it had put on weight, as the minimum allowed by the regulations was 650 kilos (1433 lbs). Eight cars were built. At the end of the season, Ferrari had won ten of the eleven races on the calendar, and if there had been a Drivers' Sports Prototype World Championship, Ferrari drivers would have occupied the first seven places.

But in 1973, the Matras appeared to spoil the party. At this point the fight with Ferrari became a battle between nations. One of the blue MS 670s won on five occasions, while the Porsche Carrera RSR won twice. At Spa it was John Wyer's Mirage which came out on top. In 1973 fortune only smiled twice on the Ferrari 312 PB, with its 450 horsepower, its 2340 mm (7'8") wheelbase and longer front end – at Monza and at the Nürburgring. There were faults in the design which showed themselves in a tendency to understeer excessively; however, nobody but the drivers would admit to this.

The twelve-cylinder engine with the wide 180-degree V angle was capable of up to 450 bhp. The 312 PB, standing on 13-inch wheels, weighed in with only 650 kilograms (1433 lbs).

365 GTC/4

The 365 GTC/4 was a Ferrari which appealed to the more mature enthusiast, according to *Road & Track* in July 1972. This model was presented at the 1971 Geneva Show and stood as the central point of the three-pronged strategy of the company which, since 1966, had stated that there should be a sporty two-seater, a comfortable four-seater and, between the two, a high performance coupé providing a high level of comfort for two.

However, the GTC/4 did have a rudimentary back seat, which could be used as an additional luggage area, especially with the seat back folded down.

Designed by Pininfarina, it combined curves and angles with wedge-shaped elements like the triangular side windows above the rear wheels. Some cynical critics pointed out similarities with the Datsun 240 Z. But a second glance was all it took to see the attraction and originality of its shape. The very long flat bonnet was made possible by the engine layout, which had six double-bodied Webers located on its side rather than in the middle of the V, unlike the Daytona configuration. This layout not only made it easier to meet the United States emission control regulations but also served to lower the centre of gravity. The 365 GTC/4 destined for the North American market was also identifiable by the four small side lights. Following the current trend, all superfluous chrome had been removed. A thin lip of synthetic material was used to protect the radiator grille and the headlights against light impact. The lip was painted matt black as were the rear bumpers. This was also the colour of the pods that held the four round dials in the driver's line of sight, as well as four further gauges slightly angled on a console which was also home to the gear lever. Unlike the Daytona, the five speed gearbox was attached directly

The Ferrari 365 GTC/4 was a classical Gran Turismo with 2+2 seats and a proud 340 bhp – the Maranello sports car for the mature enthusiast, as it were.

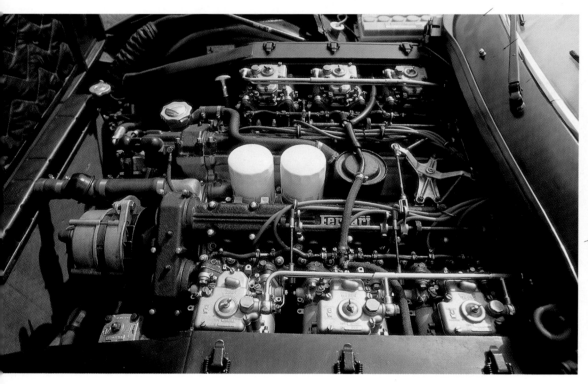

to the engine. In a strange case of shyness similar to Rolls-Royce, there was no official record of the horsepower developed by the V12 engine. "Sufficient", was the only word used, which actually meant 320 for the American version and 340 for the mature enthusiasts in other parts of the globe. For those who were not ascetics, the car was fitted with air conditioning, a system for adjusting the ride height taken from the 365 GT 2+2, as well as power steering and servo assisted brakes as standard.

Road & Track gave the front ventilated discs a real pounding, stating that after several heavy brakings the effort required on the pedal could increase by 20 percent. But as for the $ 27,500 needed to acquire a 365 GTC/4, they were more understanding – a work of art is priceless.

The interior of the 365 GTC/4 presents itself in the typical style of the early 1970s. The driver's wellbeing was taken care of by the air conditioning, while six Weber double carburetors fed the 4.4-litre large twelve-cylinder.

365 GT4 BB
BB 512
BB 512i

Drivers of the 1963 250 LM had already felt the warm air of a 12 cylinder on the back of their necks. But these cars were a limited production run and aimed primarily at competition. One had to wait a while longer for the mid-engined concept to find its way into a road car. In truth, this was not so much a revolution as an evolution, which followed a logical progression. Ferrari's customers had long been asking for this configuration, which took its identity from sports cars such as the 512 S, 512 M, and 312 PB. These last were powered by 180 degree V engines, so that they were flat, and bore the name "boxer".

This name and method of construction was reprised for the 365 GT4 BB (Berlinetta Boxer) which made its first public appearance as a prototype at the 1971 Turin show. Two years later, with only slight modifications, production began at the Scaglietti plant.

Pininfarina had done his homework. While the Lamborghini Countach displayed angular looks and a restless silhouette allowing man and machine to get their elixir of life, called oxygen, the BB boasted pure and tranquil lines. The artifice required to enable the engine to breathe had been carefully integrated into the whole – including for example, the NACA inlets located just in front of the rear wheels. When first announced, the BB nevertheless had to make its mark against the Daytona, which was the apotheosis of classic design and worshipped as such.

The Pininfarina bodywork presented itself with clear, calm lines.

Against the backdrop of the oil crisis, the BB constituted a slap in the face to all parsimonious accountants. All the more so because, for a price of SFr 117,500, one had to settle for a car that one needed to make allowances for, when it came to ownership. One sharp-tongued critic pointed out that in order to travel with luggage, one had to send it on ahead with a servant in a Range Rover. In the case of a puncture, anyone who had to make his way to the nearest Ferrari dealer, using the narrow spare wheel, would discover that there is a very thin line between the sublime and the ridiculous.

At the 1976 Paris Salon, the BB was suddenly named 512, even though the history to which it referred was less than glorious. The engine had increased in size from 4390 cc to 4942 cc, but it had lost 20 horsepower, settling at 360, albeit available at lower revs.

The 365 GT4 BB presented in 1971 possessed a mid-engine with a 180-degree V angle, which was falsely termed Boxer.

The 512 BB had dry sump lubrication. Its rear end was longer and wider to accommodate the imposing Michelin XWX 225/70 VR 15 tyres. Two sets of two rear lights replaced the previous six; and two double exhaust pipes replaced the original six on the first BB. Finally, a discrete spoiler graced the front end.

As from the 1981 Frankfurt show, the four triple Webers were replaced with a Bosch K-Jetronic injection system, which caused a drop of 20 horsepower but had no effect on the heavy fuel consumption. The unconditional Ferrari fans were hard hit by these changes.

From fall 1981 a Bosch mechanical gasoline injection (K-Jetronic), as used for example in the VW Golf GTI, took over the fuel provision.

365 GT4 2+2
400i
412

If every road-going Ferrari is a racing car to which has been added a degree of comfort, luxury and civilisation for its passengers, then this path would reach its summit with the 1972 365 GT4 2+2, and during its seventeen years in production this process would be pushed to its limit.

The car offered up by Pininfarina at the 1972 Paris Salon was seen as treachery by the Ferrari fundamentalists: a 2+2 coupé, whose serious lines hid a conventional structure: front-engined, rear wheel drive. The fact that its power output dropped progressively to 310 horsepower before returning to its original 340 at the end of its career, shows that this descendant of the noble dynasty of Maranello had a rather docile nature. Under a classical and timeless body were found the mechanics of the GTC/4, but with the wheelbase extended by 150 mm (6") to 2700 mm (8'10").

In 1976, in Paris as usual, the purists were affronted yet again. The 400A, the evolutionary phase of the big coupé, featuring a 4823 cc engine instead of the previously used 4390 cc unit, was fitted as standard with a three speed automatic box, with a torque converter made by General Motors. The five speed box was offered as a GT option.

Its looks had hardly changed. A spoiler had been added at the front, and the group of six rear lights had been reduced to four. The Rudge wheels had been replaced with five stud rims, and the front seats moved forward to allow access to the rear.

The 365 GT4 2+2 appeared in the Olympic year of 1972 – a large, timeless, and elegant coupé with an almost limousine-like silhouette and classical front engine with rear-wheel drive.

In the meantime, Ferrari technicians had spawned another revolution in as much as the V12's fuel supply was now controlled by a Bosch injection system. The result was shown in Paris in 1979. The use of simple fuel rails and an electronic box in place of the imposing double-bodied Weber 38 DCOEs left a gaping hole under the bonnet. The letter "i" bore witness to this evolution. The addition of a suspension levelling system at the rear was another innovation. The last 400i was sold in February 1985. It was black with a beige interior and was fitted with additional air conditioning. The automatic gearbox was well accepted. Out of 1810 Ferrari 400s built, only 571 had a manual gearbox. This series reached its peak at the Geneva Show from 7th to 17th March 1985, with the presentation of the 412, the first Ferrari Grand Tourer to be fitted with anti-lock brakes. As with all the GT models, it was available in eighteen

colours. The 119 cc increase in capacity was almost imperceptible, as were the modifications to the bodywork. The front and rear bumpers were colour-coded with the bodywork; rear view mirrors, skirts and window frames painted black. The factory documentation also pointed out that the boot had been slightly raised. These changes were hard to spot, but given the intimidating and majestic looks of the 412, this was of little consequence.

The 365 bore three rear lights per side at the beginning of its career, the last version, the 412, made do with two succinct lamps on its clear rear.

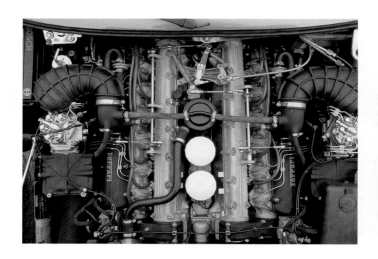

The 412, the final evolutionary development of the 365, appeared in March 1985 and was the first Ferrari with an anti-locking braking system (ABS). A Bosch mechanical gasoline injection system (K-Jetronic) took over responsibility for fuel mix preparation.

Dino 308 GT4

The fact that after twenty years of uninterrupted collaboration with Pininfarina, Ferrari entrusted the design of a production car to Bertone, was quite surprising. Even more so as the reasons for this decision were shrouded in secrecy. Perhaps Fiat, in its role of guardian, did not want to offend the other master coachbuilder of Grugliasco. Maybe the fact that in the last five years, Nuccio Bertone had provided bodywork for twelve mid-engined cars was the reason, or perhaps it was the fact he had been tempted by the challenge of squaring the circle by building a four-seater with rear-mounted engine.

Whatever the reason, his interpretation of this concept made its debut at the 1973 Paris Salon as the Dino 308 GT4. Three years later the American magazine *Road & Track* expressed a commonly held opinion, that while the success of the looks of the car were open to debate, it was a fact that the occupants had nothing to complain about. The strongly raked windscreen began from a stocky trunk bonnet. The extensions of the rear pillars were angled so that they ended at the uppermost part of the truncated rear end. The black polyester bumpers looked as though they would have difficulty resisting the

slightest knock, while during the day, the headlights were hidden behind covers no bigger than the lights themselves.

Between the two axles, separated by 2550 mm (8'4"), Bertone had placed the front seats very far forward, which allowed enough room for two more seats, which could comfortably accommodate two school-children sitting normally, and with rather more difficulty one adult sitting crosswise, although it would easily swallow excess baggage. Not that this was really necessary, as there was a space behind the engine equivalent to 188 litres (6⅔ cu.ft.), while under

The Dino 308 GT4 was not fitted out by company designer Pininfarina, but by his competitor Nuccio Bertone, also of Turin. The drive was provided by a three-litre V8 aggregate, while, inside, two children could travel in the rear emergency seating.

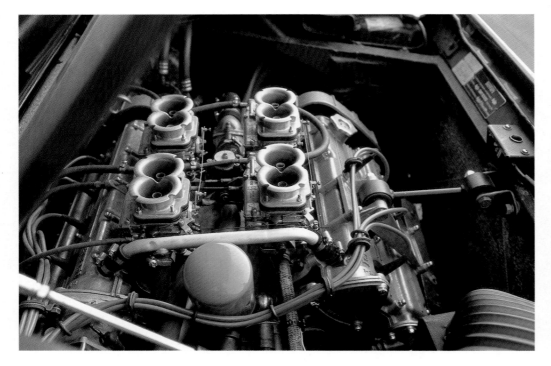

The triangular air intake for the engine room behind the second side window was characteristic of the Dino 308 GT4. The eight-cylinder aggregate operated well hidden at the rear and at right angles to the driving direction.

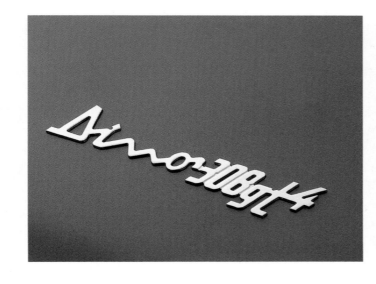

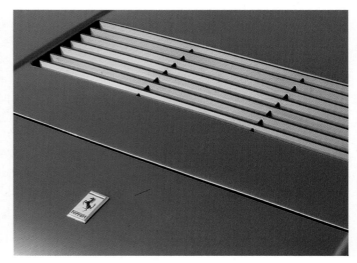

the bonnet was located a small spare wheel for situations which were probably best avoided.

The work of the engineer Franco Rocchi, the 90 degree V8, was transversally mounted. A perfect example of compactness, it was directly attached to the five speed gearbox and the differential, the whole unit fitting neatly into a small space. As with the boxer engine, the four overhead camshafts were driven by toothed belts, which were quieter than the chains used on the V12s.

In March 1975 the 208 GT4 made its entrance alongside the 308. This model had a two litre, 170 horsepower engine and was built exclusively for the Italian market, where owners of large capacity cars were heavily taxed. The differences to the three litre version were insignificant. At the most one could observe the removal of the fog lights and a slightly bigger opening for the radiator.

As from May 1976, with his infinite indulgence, the Commendatore allowed the Dino the right to wear the Ferrari family name. It is true that this noble inscription had already been seen on its rocker cover, as the 308 GT4 showed its true identity by its performance rather than its looks.

308 GTB
308 GTS
328 GTB
328 GTS

Bella macchina." In 1976 the German magazine, *auto motor und sport,* had recourse to this Italian phrase to express its enthusiasm for the model which had made its debut at the 1975 Paris Salon. The 308 GTB, fitted with a three litre engine, was at the start of a career which was to last almost 15 years, during which time 21,678 cars would be built; the absolute company record in terms of production.

At Maranello, where time moves slowly, the industrial revolution had thus begun. To produce the 308 GTB Pininfarina used mechanical components from the 308 GT4 and had taken his stylistic inspiration from the 246 GT and the 365 GT4 BB. The delicate touches he added were enough to disguise this fact when seen at first glance. The car was as beautiful as a Michelangelo sculpture. However, the fact that the bodywork was plastic was not well received by the customers, which is why, after a first run of 808 cars, Scaglietti switched to metal after April 1977. That same year, the GTS spider appeared, whose three litre engine was also transversally mounted. It, too, had a meagre boot with 155 litre (5½ cu.ft.) capacity, right at the back, and the small spare wheel was located under the bonnet, with the removable roof to protect the occupants from the excesses of the sun's rays fitting behind the seats.

Bella Macchina – *the Ferrari 308 GTB was a successful mixture of the 246 GT and the 365 BB. It was immediately an inspiration and developed into a bestseller in Ferrari's program.*

Over 21,000 examples left the Maranello works between its debut at the 1975 Paris Car Salon and termination of production in 1990. The simple elegance of the Pininfarina bodywork is timeless.

Two triangular laminated plates replaced the rear side windows and the left-hand one housed the fuel filler.

From the autumn of 1980, the adoption of a Bosch K-Jetronic injection system in place of the four DNCF double-bodied Eduardo Weber carburettors would tame the ardour of the V8, with the power dropping from 255 to 214 horsepower. This displeased the *ferraristi,* for whom a power reduction was a crime against the Ferrari idea. However, two years later, this fault was corrected, at least partially, with the adoption of a 32 valve head, which not only boosted power back to 240 horses but also increased the smoothness of the engine. This model was identifiable by the *quattrovalvole* badge on the boot.

The Spider always attracted more attention than the Berlinetta. In July 1985, out of 12,343 cars produced so far, 8004 were GTS's. The same applied to the 328

which took up the running after the Frankfurt show in 1985. Engine size had been increased to 3186 cc with 270 horsepower. At the same time it had grown a little: 25 mm (10") longer, 8 mm (0.3") taller and 10 mm (0.4") wider, as had its track. The front end took its inspiration from the Testarossa. The vents behind the headlight covers had gone, while the grille had grown in size. The configuration of the lights had changed, and the black front spoiler, which included an additional air intake, had expanded; the interior had been changed as had the layout of the gauges. This led to the handbrake lever being exiled to the left side of the driver. From the outside, only the most expert onlooker could recognize this version, whose owners had to make do with only 155 horsepower. But this weakness would become a *tour de force* after a two stage modification. In 1982 power was upped to 220 horsepower thanks to a KKK turbo, and in 1986 the car gained a further 34 horsepower with the adoption of an additional radiator for the turbo-charged air.

The 308 GTB mutated in 1985 into the 328 GTB. Here the eight-cylinder worked with a capacity of 3.2 litres, and the GTS called Spider was the declared love of 328 customers.

Mondial 8
Mondial 3.2
Mondial t
Mondial Cabriolet

Introduced in the spring of 1980 at the Geneva Show, the Mondial 8 filled the gap left by the disappearance of the 308 GT4. Its name recalled a glorious page in the history of the marque. Mondial had been the name give to a two litre sports car that had made its debut in the 12 Hours of Casablanca back in December 1953.

This time, the difficult task of designing a car with a 2650 mm (8'8") wheelbase that could accept a four-seater body and a V8 fell to Pininfarina. The master coachbuilder did a good job but everyone agreed that it was the inner values of the Mondial that were exceptional.

The smell of the Connolly leather trim, the two-way adjustable steering wheel, air conditioning, central locking, electric windows and rear view mirrors, as well as a control system that would indicate, for example, that a door had not been properly closed: all these signs of civilisation partly made up for the fact that sitting in the second row was not very comfortable. But there was no doubt about it; the three litre V8 behind the rear seats definitely spoke the noble language of Maranello.

The voluminous air intakes in front of the rear wheels shaped side elevation of the Mondial, which came onto the market as the successor to the 308 GT4.

In July 1982 it was fitted with four valves per cylinder, which boosted its power by 26 to 240 horsepower, which could be felt from 2000 rpm and really kicked in at 5500 rpm. The Cabriolet, shown at the Brussels show in January 1983, was at first only destined for the North American market. It was the first topless Ferrari since the Daytona Spider. Its shape was tinged with honest aggression, even with the roof on, and it turned out to be a success.

At Frankfurt in 1985, the Mondial was shown, just like its sister model the 328, with a new 270 horsepower engine, identifiable by the 3.2 badge on the rear. Cosmetic changes concerned the radiator grille, the headlights and the spoiler. The bumpers were colour-matched to the body, the style of wheel was simplified, and the whole car was 45 mm (1.8") shorter, 5 mm (0.2") wider and 25 mm (1") lower.

Pininfarina was once again responsible for the Mondial design, however, the enthusiasm for the form of the 2+2-seater was limited.

From the Geneva show of 1989, the door handles were also the car colour, and the main lights and side vents were smaller.

But the most important change occurred under the bonnet. The engine, increased in size to 3405 cc, put out 300 horsepower and was positioned longitudinally, while the gearbox was transversally mounted with a linkage to the clutch fitted between the two main shafts.

This design reprised the one used on the famous Grand Prix single-seater Tipo 312 T from the seventies. It offered three major advantages: the engine and therefore the centre of gravity was 130 mm (5") lower; the length could be reduced; and maintenance was simpler. Automatic adjustment of the damper movement had three possible modes to choose from, but generally drivers would select the softest and did not touch it again.

The Mondial t was also available as a full cabriolet. Its
technical finesses included the cross-mounted transmission
placed behind the lengthways-mounted engine.

288 GTO

It was being whispered that, even at Maranello, the routine of the production line had become the norm when, on 28th February 1984 to be precise, at the Geneva show, a stinging reply to this criticism appeared in the shape of the 288 GTO. On the strength of its badge alone, which had passed into myth and legend, it had to be brutally powerful, brutally quick and brutally beautiful. And desperately expensive – it was priced at DM 260,000 in the German catalogue. But it was impossible to buy one at this price. Even before production had started in July of that year, the entire batch of 273 cars had already been sold, and the price had been a question of small supply and big demand.

The resemblance to the 308 GTB which had formed the basis for the design was only skin deep. At the front were a bigger spoiler and a different layout for the lights. On the sides were upswept rear view mirrors and muscular wings as well as horizontal air vents under the doors. At the rear there were oblique vents behind the wheels, evoking memories of the old GTO. The back end of the car swept up energetically revealing an impressive set of exhausts.

This visual inferno was the work of Pininfarina stylist Leonardo Fioravanti, while the liberal application of fibreglass, Kevlar and Nomex bore witness to the philosophy of Harvey Postlethwaite, who employed these materials in 1982 on the Grand Prix cars of the marque. The exhausts of the V8, which had been reduced to 2855 cc for homologation reasons, intruded right up between the very firm GTO seats. The engine was mounted longitudinally and even the wheelbase stretched to 2450 mm (8 ft) had not contained its expansionist outlook.

It bore a great name: GTO. However, this 288 GTO shone not in racing sport, but was the fastest road-Ferrari of the time. This beauty powered by a biturbo V8 engine was capable of just over 300 kph (185 mph).

The subtle rear spoiler of the 288 GTO optimized the tread pressure on the rear wheels, only the cult abbreviation on the trunk betrayed the enormous potential of this sports car.

Under the ribbed bonnet reigned mechanical violence and perfect symmetry. Each bank of cylinders had two camshafts, 16 valves and a Japanese IHI turbo, as well as a huge intercooler. There was never any doubting the factory's claimed 400 horsepower.

Klaus Westrup felt the same way, writing in *auto motor und sport.* He affirmed that the background noise unleashed when the driver turned the ignition key and hit the floor with his right foot was absolutely diabolical. It was impossible to tell if it was a four, a six, an eight or a twelve cylinder, which just behind one let out trumpet blasts, growled, screamed and whistled with but one voice.

The writer also questioned the wisdom of the law, which basically allowed any rich driver who had just passed his test to be let loose and alone at the wheel of such a beast.

The eight-cylinder engine in classical V 90 degree configuration hid itself under the two powerful intercoolers of the Stuttgart specialists Behr.

Testarossa
512 TR
F512 M

Considering the number of aerodynamic aids of all types on display at the 1984 Paris Salon, one observer wrote that the Testarossa did not need a wing because it was one. He thus awarded the latest creation from Pininfarina's Studi e Ricerche S.p.A. at Cambiano a flattering certificate. However, not everything was perfect. As remarked by the journalist

and former racer Giancarlo Baghetti, whose love for the noble cars of Maranello is unquestioned, above 250 kph (155 mph) the front end of the Testarossa had a wicked habit of getting too light. A design that took its inspiration from part of an aerofoil; at two metres (6'7"), almost twice as wide as its height; side with large grooves designed to channel the air to the radia-tors: such were the characteristic lines of the Testa-rossa. The huge 180 degree V 12 engine stretched out behind the passengers, similar in principle to the one in the BB 512, with the difference that there were four valves per cylinder and that it had 390 horsepower. In memory of the old Testa Rossa the cam covers were painted red. The successor to this model, the 512 TR,

The Testarossa of the 1980s accommodated its twelve cylinders in the vehicle's middle, sucking in air to breathe through it side gills.

went into production in the second half of 1991 and was shown at the Los Angeles Show in January 1992. It had 38 more horsepower, weighed 40 kilos (88 lbs) less, the engine was lowered by 30 mm (1.2"), it was shod with lower profile tyres and had improved brakes.

Pininfarina stylist Lorenzo Ramaciotti had given it the look of the Ferrari family of the nineties, with a trapezoidal-shaped grille with rounded corners flanked by bigger open lights, underlined by a discrete spoiler. The horizontal line was a constant in the design, in particular around the back of the car where the rear lights appeared to be almost hidden by the black grille whereas the black air vents in the extensions of the roof had been removed. Overall, however, there had been no radical changes to the shape and this fidelity to the original lines had the added advantage of not requiring new manufacturing tools.

Ferrari took up a great name once again with the term "Testarossa": with the 500 Testa Rossa of 1956, there had already been a vehicle with red-painted cylinder heads. The small picture on the right imposingly illustrates how the air circulation was controlled for the powerful V12-cylinder engine. The lower illustration shows very clearly that Pininfarina had this time chosen the horizontal as the main design theme.

The up until now last development stage to take place under this legendary name, the F512M, emerged exactly ten years after the renewed debut of the Testarossa. The most modern technology, less weight, and, with 440 bhp, more performance provided the exclamation mark at the end of a long period of development.

A third evolution appeared in the autumn of 1994. This time the front end had been redrawn to resemble that of the F355 and the 456 GT, in other words the base model and the luxury model of the range. This meant that even the most out-and-out *ferrarista* had something to smile about.

It was a lot more than a re-styling exercise, said sales director Michele Scannavini, because it included fundamental changes. This explained the "M" for *modificata,* just as appeared on the 512 racing Berlinettas of 1971. There were four major points: a weight reduction of 18 kilos (40 lbs) thanks to a costly slimming operation; an increase of 12 horsepower; the adoption of fixed headlights carefully crafted into the bodywork; and uncovered round lights at the rear.

In these terms, progress could be seen as relying on well-tried solutions, which was often the case with Pininfarina.

The magnificent twelve-cylinder engine was an inspiration with its spontaneous performance and perfectly tuned sound. The mighty perforated brake disks behind the paddle-formed alloy wheels ensured optimal braking.

Ferrari set a totally
high-end sports car on
wheels under the simple
description F40 with its
top speed of 320 kph
(199 mph) and 478 bhp.

The stock of old model names from the glorious past was far from exhausted, but in order to celebrate the forty years of the marque which had begun with the 125 S, Ferrari created a new legend.

It was a monument to speed, to style, to performance and it was overflowing with power. F40 – that short name summed up the event, making emotions soar into the red zone on the emotional rev counter. But it is not only the 1311 proud owners of an F40 that fall prey to its magic. For to park an F40 somewhere is to return to a car covered in the fingerprints of the numerous admirers who cluster around it, in an effort to understand it better by touch.

The car that the venerable Enzo Ferrari came to unveil personally on 12th March 1987, on the stroke of midday at the Centro Civico di Maranello, was an incarnation of aggression, a menacing mixture of slopes and chasms, ploughed and riddled all over, all topped off with an impressive wing. Because above 300 kph (185 mph), air resistance is just enormous, the air flow is essential, not only to keep the car stuck to the ground, but also to cool the

mechanical components as well as the occupants before it exits the car, taking the heat with it.

From the aesthetic and pragmatic ends of the spectrum, Leonardo Fioravanti and his team in charge of styling for Pininfarina had opted for a route that favoured the bizarre and the dramatic on its way to the supreme expression of automotive beauty.

The body of the F40 was built out of noble plastics, three times stiffer and 20 per cent lighter than a similar metal structure. The tubular structure, a veritable backbone, was reinforced with Kevlar,

The noble plastic alloy bodywork of the F40 was clearly more rigid and 20 percent lighter than a comparable metal structure.

The heart of the F40 lay open for all passersby to see under the large plexiglas cover. However, the two large intercoolers optically dominated the engine room.

carbon fibre and fibreglass. Under the rear window and naked to the eye were the mechanical parts, both beautiful and intimidating to look at. It was a calculated effect. To hell with diplomacy, the F40 was aimed at a new, almost unknown level, pushing the physical and technical boundaries to their limit. What is more, it was superior to its average driver in every way.

Getting on board was difficult. To begin with, a structural cross-member got in your way and had to be overcome. But once installed in the bucket seats, of which there were three available options to suit all sizes, the level of comfort was surprisingly high.

Pressing a rubberised button unleashed a hurricane behind the passenger's ears, followed by a whole range of sounds from the strange to the diabolical, making all conversation impossible with the excep-tion of the odd monosyllabic comment. At maximum revs in first and second gears, clouds of blue smoke would pour out from around the large Michelin 335/35 ZR 17 tyres, as they showed their displeasure at being tortured in this way by laying down snaking black tracks on the tarmac. And after a mere eleven seconds, the 200 kph (124 mph) barrier had been rapidly swallowed up.

The atmosphere in the cockpit was austere, with absolutely no artificial embellishment. It was a monk's cell. Fitting air conditioning was essential to survival if one wanted to avoid being cooked alive.

But the lucky driver and passenger of an F40 will-ingly accepted all these hardships. The chance of getting acquainted with one of the three most exciting motoring experiences of the century easily warrants making a few concessions.

The F40's drive system had an abundance of power: eight cylinders, a three-litre capacity, four valves per cylinder, two turbochargers, two intercoolers, 478 bhp at 7000 rpm. That's enough!

For the absolute purist Ferrari delivered the F40 GT Competizione. Its few owners could enjoy narrow bucket seats, perforated aluminium pedals, and other racing components. It was indeed a pure driving machine.

348 GTB
348 GTS
348 Spider

It took up the reins of the bestselling 328, which meant it had to face certain responsibilities. But the signs were favourable. The market was going through a boom period. Cheques would arrive at Maranello from passionate enthusiasts and from speculators. Even before the car appeared, the waiting list and the order book were full well into the nineties. It was in this climate that the two newcomers made their first appearance as a duo. Unlike 1977, when a delay in producing the GTS version was helpful in drumming

up interest in the 308, no such tension-creating tactics were required this time.

At first they were called tb and ts; b for Berlinetta, s for Spider, even though the latter was actually a Targa body. The t signified *trasversale* and referred to the transversally-mounted gearbox located behind the longitudinally-mounted engine, which was based on the 3405 cc V8 that powered the Mondial. At first it developed 300 horsepower, which was upped to 320 from the autumn of 1993. This configuration, derived

from the single-seaters of the seventies, had the advantage of bringing together the maximum weight possible in between the front and rear axles.

Without detracting from the skill and merit of Ferrari and Pininfarina, who once again hail managed to create an irreproachable symbiosis between the twin imperatives of form and function, the structure they had decided on also influenced the overall shape. With its short front overhang, its spoilers and its skirts, the 348 was basically a stocky looking car, with

Success brings its obligations – the 348 superseded the 328 bestseller and went on to write the Ferrari success story of the 1990s. With the right intuition, Ferrari and Pininfarina met the taste of their well-off clients.

A targa version with the abbreviation "ts" came onto the market at the same time as the closed model; a policy that was just as unusual as it was successful at the time.

its lateral grooves and slats arranged further forward than on the Testarossa or Mondial.

The ts differed from the Berlinetta in terms of its fibreglass, steel-reinforced roof weighing seven kilos (15 lbs). When removed, the roof fitted behind the seats. This measure reduced leg room by ten centimetres (4").

All the same, the 348 offered sufficient space for two to travel in admirable yet close comfort. The baggage space situated below the front lid would not under any circumstances have had room for three people's luggage, and in general it was preferable to fill it with made-to-measure suitcases, finished in yellow leather and available at a price that would buy you a nice second-hand car.

To general admiration, the 348 Spider was revealed in February 1993 in a smart part of Beverly Hills. This was the second new Ferrari to be shown in the space of just five months; the other one being the 456 GT. This was a true act of courage in times of economic hardship. Lorenzo Ramaciotti, the Pininfarina director, resorted to a few delicate understatements when presenting this creation. He said that it was always difficult producing a cabriolet from a pretty closed car, as there was always the risk that the bulk of the original vehicle would be too much in evidence.

His worries were totally unfounded. The hood blended in marvellously well with the lines of the car. And when it was folded down and slid into the space provided for this purpose, and it was hidden under a stud-fastening cover, the amount of material still visible was limited to a small bump in which could be detected a suggestion of the shape of the roof with its supports angled to the rear.

This cabriolet was so well designed that it seemed to be declaring war on all the other cabriolets in the world. The winner of this war was easy to predict.

*Much of the 348's form
language is reminiscent of
the Testarossa: the slats
above the rear lights, the air
outlets of the rear hood –
all in all the emphasis on
the horizontal.*

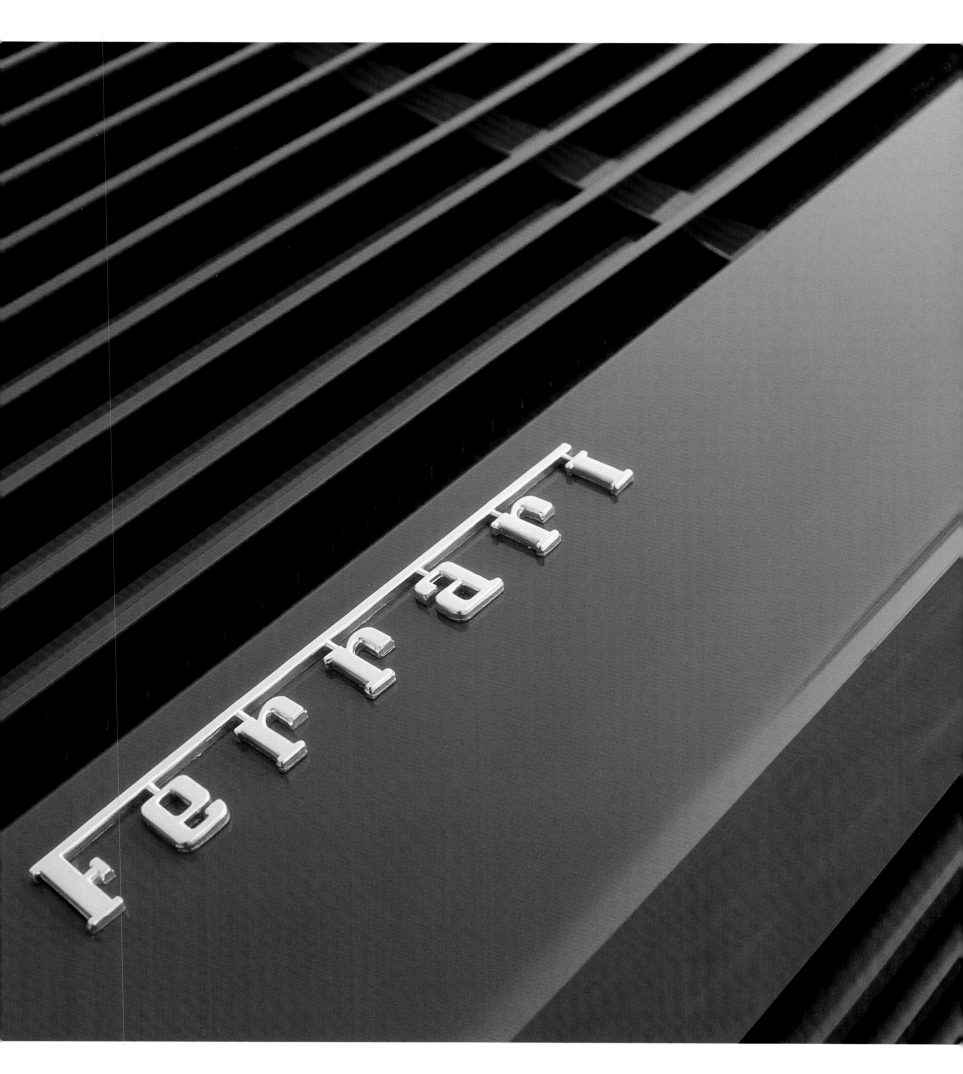

The 3.4-litre and 320 bhp
eight-cylinder provided
a vehement thrust for
the Spider as well.
Pleasure in one of its most
beautiful forms!

456 GT
456 GTA
456M GT

Dignified, free of excess, as refined as one could wish for and ready to pick up the baton of the Ferrari Grand Tourers which seemed to be extinct with the disappearance of the 412 in 1989 – this was how the 456 GT presented itself, the incarnation of unalloyed classicism, at the Paris show held from 8th to 18th October 1992.

Under the direction of Amedeo Felisa, it had been developed by the GT department on the instructions of senior management. As to its styling, that was the work of the *Centro Studi e Ricerche,* the holy of holies at Pininfarina, under the leadership of Lorenzo Ramaciotti.

With obvious joy the Turin maestros had dug deep in the accessories box to find beautiful yet tried and tested solutions. The face of the bulky coupé, on which the *cavallino rampante* emblem pranced no less than fifteen times in total, betrayed its genetic association with the 512 TR and the 348. The sides revealed links with those of the F40 and the Mythos, while the massive rear end took its inspiration from the Daytona.

Not a single wing came to upset its purity of line. A movable deflector was integrated into the rear bumper, however. An electronic device would modify its angle at speeds above 110 kph (68 mph)

and, logically, it would return to its original position below 80 kph (50 mph).

It was prudent not to open the doors of the 456 GT too quickly as the windows needed time to detach themselves, with a slight shudder, from their sealed surround. The relatively generous interior space tended to favour the front seat occupants, while access to the rear seats was facilitated by the front seats automatically sliding forward with an electronic hum as soon as their seat backs were tipped up. A metallic black ambience prevailed in the cockpit area, with a host of rocker switches which would click into action to operate such things as the three damper settings for the suspension, or the unlocking of the fuel filler cap. The gearlever slotted into a gate to choose one of the six forward gears. So in almost any situation there was a choice of two gears, when after just a quarter turn on the ignition key, the split personality of the 456 GT began to manifest itself, part high performance saloon, part strong and dominating sports car.

While the sound deadening was effective, the 12 cylinder engine, the development of which had made more use of the computer than ever before, still made a beautiful noise, from the depths of a baritone right up to the highest pitched sharps of a soprano. It had a more than willing amount of torque: in sixth

Yet another Ferrari in the great GT tradition: a twelve-cylinder front engine and rear-wheel drive, dressed to accentuate its beautiful lines with a bodywork formed from every point of view without a blemish.

The appearance of the 456 betrayed its genetic closeness to the 512 TR and the 348. The open gearshift lever gate is typical for Ferrari.

gear at idle, the engine was ready to leap into action without showing any signs of displeasure.

The opulent standard equipment included a radio installation that was suitably complicated to operate; a set of five sienna-coloured suitcases; and a progressive power steering that made turning the wheel easier up to 70 kph (44 mph) without affecting its sensitivity to the road.

This slot in the Ferrari range was governed by its own laws, with the majority of customers opting for one of the four blue finishes available, and only a minority choosing the traditional red.

Sergio Pininfarina was especially open to customer wishes for a 456 GT automatic: "Of all the vehicles I have designed, the GTA is still my favourite car. When I drive it, I enjoy all the details which make it more and more my car." Sergio had treated himself for his private ocean blue GTA – "A" for automatic – to several of the nice extras from the "Carrozzeria Scaglietti" personalisation programme created in 1997.

Modification of the wheel suspension, bodywork and interior, bestowed in 1998 a further additive on the 456 GT: "M" for *modificata.* The letter was placed directly after the figure 456, the cylinder volume in cc.

The V12-cylinder engine, with its 442 bhp from a capacity of five and a half litres, brings the four-seater to 300 kph (185 mph) perfectly well. A classical gearshift lever gate and the return to many classical elements of styling are married to the latest technology of the time.

F333 SP

The marque's customers wanted a sports car, and so it was a pleasure for Ferrari to respond to this wish, said spokesman Giancarlo Baccini as the F333 SP was unveiled in January 1994. This pleasure had nevertheless been a long time coming, and had taken two decades to arrive while Ferrari had concentrated solely on Formula 1.

This phase of absence bore three fruits, but only for the rich amateur driver. There were three European series and an American-Canadian tour for the 348 Challenge. There were entries in the GT category for the smallest Ferrari and a limited edition of 50 cars was specially built with this in mind. And there was also the participation of the F333 SP in the WSCC (World Sports Car Championship) races run under the auspices of the International Motor Sport Association (IMSA) in the United States.

The moving forces behind this project were Ferrari North America under the presidency of Gian Luigi Buitoni and Ferrari stalwart, Giampiero Moretti, who had already won his spurs for the small black horse at the wheel of a 512 S. From the F333 SP debut at Road Atlanta in April 1994 on, he was considered part and parcel of the effort.

Usually painted red as it should be, the bodywork was made of carbon fibre and Nomex. If the need arose in the heat of battle, it could be partially removed. What is more, the carbon fibre contributed

With the F333 SP, Ferrari returned in 1994 to the sports car racing scene once more, after decades of abstinence. The racing operation was left to dedicated private teams.

to the rigidity of this two-seater, as it had been combined with aluminium to form the monocoque. The gearbox had also been mounted on the small area between the two axles. As a concession to technological evolution, the traditional gear selection pattern had been sacrificed on the altar of progress and changing to one of the five forward gears was done by means of a sequential box.

The engine, a 3997 cc, 65 degree V12 with five titanium valves per cylinder, angered the other competitors, who claimed it went against the traditions, customs and spirit of IMSA racing, in so much as this engine was not commercially available.

Gian Luigi Buitoni did not let such a trifle stand in his way, and revealed the secret that the F333 SP engine architecture was quite similar to that of the F130, which was the factory name of the future F50.

The Swiss industrialist Fredy Lienhard's Lista team started successfully with the F333 SP at the World Sports Car Series races. The four-litre engine with a performance of more than 650 bhp was, of course, a twelve-cylinder.

F355 Berlinetta · F355 GTS · F355 Spider · F355 Challenge

F355 Berlinetta
F355 GTS
F355 Spider
F355 Challenge

The Ferrari F355, unveiled on Tuesday 24th May 1994, in Berlinetta and GTS versions at Maranello by Ferrari President Luca Cordero di Montezemolo to a group of fifty hand-picked journalists, faced a dilemma. It was almost too effective, and tended to put in the shade the 512 TR, its bigger and older sister, by lapping the company's own Fiorano test track a full three seconds quicker. It was unquestionably good-looking. Sergio Pininfarina, who described his latest creation as "solid muscle", explained that cars capable of almost 300 kph (185 mph) depended to a great extent on work in the wind tunnel. As an example, the front spoiler exploited the F355's air flow in two ways. At its sides the flow was directed to the outside, in the centre, on the other hand, it was channelled under the car where it generated ground effect thanks to the flat smooth floor pan. In spite of the necessities dictated by aerodynamics, explained Pininfarina, there still were sufficient areas for creative freedom to express itself.

In fact, in a calculated move, the exterior of the 348 had been carefully retouched in an attempt to uncover the very idea of the 3 litre Ferrari as it were. The last figure of the code number 355 no longer indicated the number of cylinders. It signified, as di Montezemolo underlined, the fact that each cylinder had five valves, giving a total of 40 to a V8 weighing a mere 150 kilos (330 lbs).

Furthermore, the F355 brought together seemingly irreconcilable extremes in that it was both wilder and yet easier to tame. For example, at low speeds the driver could count on the help of power steering, which had long been considered a taboo by true enthusiasts of the marque. They felt the same about the fact that this type of Ferrari should be equipped

As the observer already suspects, the F355 Berlinetta is the legitimate successor to the 348. Sergio Pininfarina observed a "muscular sturdiness" in his latest creation.

The Spider beguiled the viewer with its unlimited openness, and the driver with a hardly beatable synthesis of its over foaming temperament and the erotic sound sequences of its potent eight cylinders.

with suspension that could be set for comfort or for speed. The primeval cry of past generations had definitely been replaced by classical music, a *sinfonia concertante* between *adagio* and *allegro molto, piano* and *fortissimo,* that fitted in perfectly with the new Ferrari image.

Those who felt that the F355 had become too soft could change at least two points to strip it of some luxury. It was possible to have the power steering removed and to specify, as an option, ascetic bucket seats made from carbon fibre, instead of the comfortable ones fitted as standard.

Cabriolet owners, who had to make do with the previous model for a further year, could only smile in commiseration at such alternatives. All they had to do was turn a central locking mechanism above the

windscreen, pull back the roof by hand until an alarm sounded, and then press a switch. In a blink of an eye the soft top would fold up and disappear into a recess in front of the engine compartment. As the roof disappeared, so did any thought of performance, speed and acceleration. Because in the world of the cabriolet, togetherness is regulated by milder legislation.

And whoever entertained sporting ambitions could acquire the F355 Challenge competition version to tussle on the racetrack with the like-minded for a trophy. In 1997 Ferrari fitted out the F355, under the name of 355 F1, with an electro-hydraulic transmission borrowed from the Monoposto. And so the paddles behind the steering wheel, first tested in Nigel Mansell's F1 Ferrari in 1989, finally found their way into a road car.

A capacity of 3.5 litres, 380 bhp, five valves per cylinder – that's the bare data of one of the most rpm friendly engines of the 1990s. Sober functionality is provided by the interior.

F50

It was Piero Ferrari's idea to build a "Barchetta" like the 1947 125 S, but one that made use of all the technical progress discovered during this journey through time, around the world from Maranello to Maranello.

Ferrari's dream Ferrari was given its world première at the Geneva show in March 1995, but all the indications were that it had arrived at the wrong time. It was launched too early, as its model number anticipated the company's fiftieth birthday. It also arrived too late, however, as it had been expected as early as 1993. Luca di Montezemolo admitted that the 456 GT, F512 M and F355 models had been the money-spinners. Therefore they were given priority over the F50 supercar, of which, in parsimonious fashion, only 349 would be built.

But which version to keep in the air-conditioned garage? The Berlinetta or the Spider? The dilemma was easy to solve, as it was both at the same time. With a little bit of practice the roof could be fitted in just half an hour. All that needed to be done was to remove the roll-over bars and the two rounded protuberances behind the passengers, that Pininfarina had designed by taking his inspiration from the sports racing cars of the fifties.

According to di Montezemolo, in essence this car was a Formula 1 that one could drive to the shops. This was just a little bit optimistic. Climbing into the somewhat inhospitable cockpit, one first had to

There were only 349 produced: the F50 is the ultimate sports car for road traffic. Ferrari president Luca di Montezemolo characterized the F50 as a Formula 1 vehicle with which you could also fetch your bagels.

The F50 appears to literally suck up the road. Aerodynamics, optimized in the wind tunnel, produce a vacuum and tread pressure that ensure stable driving even at speeds of 325 kph (200 mph).

negotiate two large sills before sinking into the composite construction bucket seats, available in two sizes. Once inside, the surroundings were austere, apart from the incongruity of air-conditioning. The rev counter and speedometer were analogue, while fuel gauge, oil pressure and temperature, water temperature, as well as a gear indicator, were all digitally displayed. Pervading everything was the smell of Connolly leather.

Under this thin veneer of civilisation was hidden a pure racing car, with air intakes carved into the sides, in similar fashion to the Grand Prix car of the day, the 412 T2. The windscreen had a strong curve to it, similar to the Group C cars. The shape increased downforce behind the cockpit area, and a raised wing dominated the rear. The underside of the car, which swept up towards the rear, was sculpted to provide a diffuser effect, so that as speed increased, the F50 stuck ever more firmly to the road.

The weight was reduced by the use of high technology materials with wheel hubs and con rods made of titanium and wheels constructed from magnesium. The chassis and body were made of carbon fibre, truly the black gold of the end of the century, and weighed only 100 kilos (220 lbs). It was baked in an oven at incredibly high temperatures after a long and complex manufacturing process.

This approach meant that the car was rigid enough for the V12 engine and the transmission components to be used as load-bearing structures. The engine had aluminium pistons and a seven bearing crankshaft. The block was cast allowing for thinner walls and compact dimensions. The maximum torque of 470 Newton metres was attained at 6500 rpm, and the engine hit its peak of 520 horsepower at 8500 rpm. The pushrod suspension was supplemented by horizontally mounted springs and dampers. Here again, the F50 took its inspiration from the 412 T2.

The result of this show of force was a Fiorano lap time which was a staggering four seconds quicker than the legendary F40. Each second represents another red thread in the tapestry of the myth that is Ferrari, onto which millions of motorists all over the world project their keenest wishes and dreams.

An open gate gear change with carbon gear knob, a twelve-cylinder engine with 520 bhp and a bewitching sound, as well as generously dimensioned brake disks, are a few of the components that ennoble the F50 as a motorized work of art.

550 Maranello
550 Barchetta
575 M Maranello

Apart from a few exceptions, the prancing horse's model classifications have grown out of engine volume and cylinder number. A small mathematical problem arose with the 456 GT in 1996, for the "pot" content had already been awarded to another splendid steed, similarly equipped, which was already scraping its hooves to leave the stable. A clever marketing brain at Ferrari came up with the number 550 by using a simple formula: the total volume of the 12 cylinders

rounded to the nearest full hundred and divided by 10, in order to remain in the three figure area. A rather disdainful number incapable of expressing the power and beauty of the classy coupé with the long motor bonnet, ergo the melodious name of the stud farm's location, Maranello, was added. *Basta!*

Despite the entire sporting aura with which Ferrari emphasised in all its official statements that a vehicle with a front engine could by all means take on a mid-engined creation – a sideswipe at Lamborghini – travelling comfort is not neglected in this Grand-Tourer. For longer, pleasurable excursions where nothing disturbs but the fuel consumption, the softer alternative damper setting is recommended. A set of travel bags with the Ferrari name, firmly strapped to the shelf behind the seats, belong to the luxuriant interior. There is even room for a suitcase, at the rear in front of the spare tyre.

It carries the 456 GT genes, but the 550 Maranello, which had its debut in 1996, is the more sporting alternative with its shorter wheelbase. Its Pininfarina bodywork fills with enthusiasm from every viewing angle.

Even though a sprint of 100 kph (62 mph) in 4.4 seconds and a top speed of 320 kph (199 mph) can hardly be called modest, a watchful eye was kept on the competition, response at the ready. In 2002 an increase in displacement to 5748 cc drew even more potential out of the V12, no less than 515 bhp. Due to this and the by now optional rocker switching, the repositioning of the instrumentation with a large central tachometer and minimal further face-liftings, the Maranello received the new designation 575 – following the above formula – and the usual Ferrari identification code for modifications "M". *Tutto chiaro?*

The 575 M reaches a sprint result of 4.25 seconds with conventional gear changing and 4.2 with the hydraulic automatic – according to the manufacturer's specifications. To tear off like that, whether manually or with the rocker switch impulses, requires routine and sure instincts. Some Maranello drivers who are not acquainted with the transaxle system have to grit their teeth with the 6 speed gears, as the gearwheels brutishly interlock with each other at high revs. A robust driving style on a winding stretch requires steering wheel correction during gear change, as the Maranello's rear begins to waggle. After all, the 575 M

The Maranello mutated in the new millennium to the 575 M with even more power (515 bhp) and a subtle optical retouching. Thanks to a perfectly balanced aerodynamic the 325 kph (202 mph) fast Bello di Maranello can decline the use of spoilers.

weighs in at 1730 kg (3815 lbs) – despite the aluminium bodywork welded to the steel frame with a special alloy – a body mass that needs to be kept under control.

To make a powerful lightweight muscle-packet out of it was the task of Ferrari's sport department. Despite rollover cage, racing tyre width, complete aerodynamic fittings with cantilevered rear spoiler and an increased engine capacity of 6 litres, the weight of the competition version, known as GTC, sank to the FIA's minimum of 1100 kg (2425 lbs). 605 bhp already at 6300 rpm promise longevity, and then a torque of 730 Newton meter at 5200 revs – what a virile little chap!

Irrespective of engine or body form – the powerful and elegant 575 Maranello satisfies in all respects.
Gear switching is carried out with filigree rocker switches on the steering wheel – as in Formula 1. Passé is the typical open gearshift gate.

At the prelude to the 2003 FIA GT Championship in Barcelona, the GTC literally sucked up its fellow competitors through its powerful air intakes, with one even set into the roof in rally style. As with Julius Caesar of old, *"Veni, vidi, vici":* a threefold victory for the Maranello team at its first battle!

They fought over the racetracks of Europe, and thrashed their opponents. Only in the land of the Belgian Gaul and on the territory of the Viking were they unsuccessful. At the end of this conflict, the drivers of three Ferrari warhorses were awarded the FIA victory laurels.

Ferrari, *in hoc signo vinces!*

Purely an object of lust – the 550 Barchetta was conceived as a vehicle for the unadulterated lust for automobile locomotion. The connoisseur behind the steering wheel enthused over the orchestral sound of the twelve-cylinder, and the almost unlimited openness.

A sporting ambience also dominates the interior. Optimally formed sports seats – naturally covered in finest leather – and four-point seat belts allow the pilot to experience directly every movement of the more than 500 bhp-strong Barchetta. The most perfect of driving pleasures.

360 Modena
360 Spider

"First of all, a car has to be dreamt", Enzo Ferrari once lectured, when discussing a new Ferrari's pleasing appearance with his coachbuilder and couturier Battista "Pinin" Farina.

When the 360 Modena, the successor to the F355, was presented in 1999, Sergio Pininfarina – son of the past master – was showered with praise for his dream-like creation, which had been endowed with a high technical specification profile. The aerodynamics of this sporty mid-engined vehicle were not to rely on additional "wings". In order to reduce the uplift caused by high speeds, Sergio consequently incorporates the under body. The maestro of functional aesthetics channels the air under the 360 to a formidable diffuser. In the mid-section of which he mounts the transmission.

Around 5400 hours of wind tunnel testing provide the aerodynamic fine finish, enabling Pininfarina's 163rd Ferrari to do without visible spoilers, apart from a small rear end edge outline. Radiators suck the airflow through side air intakes instead of through a central radiator grill, and exhale through similar, rather noisy features at the rear. The simple unadorned aluminium body displays the traditional side air inlets, obviously for Pininfarina a theme for almost endless variations: no angular corners, smoothly-led curves all the way to the rear end. You only need to bend over the rear end and the motor presents itself

Pininfarina's language of form interprets the final Ferrari of the 20th century, conforming to aspects of aerodynamics, into a formal unity.

as if in a glass showcase, inviting further inspection. Especially eye-catching: the red air manifolds with the Ferrari name. A whiff of Testarossa is discernable. The carefully thought-out air supply system dominates optically. The power unit with its most important ancillary aggregates rests in a square supporting-frame, also made of aluminium.

Employing a Bosch electronic engine management system, the 3.6-Litre-V8 with 40 valves, titanium con rods, and forged aluminium pistons reaches at 8500 rpm its top performance of 400 bhp, accompanied by a sound that swells from the initial dull roar to a high pitched scream on nearing the maximum rpm allowed. The most powerful 8-cylinder guzzler to date already reaches its torque of 373 Newton meter at 4750 rpm.

The experience of driving pleasure starts with simply sitting in the Connolly leather bucket seats, studying the round instruments of the dashboard and then concentrating on the tachometer in the middle. Most 360 drivers prefer the electro-hydraulic Tiptronic transmission, as finger wrestling with the open, aluminium manual mechanism tends to distract. The pleasure of changing gear as in a Formula 1 monoposto may cost an additional 7000 Euros, but in view of the

relatively favourable 1999 starting price of roughly 113,500 Euros, this extra is quite affordable. The sole drawback: a minute lever to operate the reverse gear has to taken into account.

Irrespective of manual or sequential operation, the six-speed transmission enjoys change when accelerating to 100 kph (62 mph) in 4.5 seconds and a kilometre (1094 yds) from standstill in 22.9 seconds. The engine's accompanying music is a feast for the ears, with which the sound output of the standard built-in hi-fi with cassette recorder or CD player acoustically cannot compete. The only comparison: playing a recording of the roar of a Formula 1 start.

Anti-slip control and two different damper settings, electronically selectable by switch, ensure optimal ground contact for the sportily designed chassis, the dual wishbones and stabilisers of which are also of aluminium. The Modena shines with its road holding in those speed areas which lie beyond normal road traffic conditions. Endless driving enjoyment up to 300 kph (185 mph) – for those who can and may – without remorse!

The relatively clinical effect of the spacious cockpit, with room for a golf bag behind the seats, is not unsettling. The "Carozzeria Scaglietti" programme

Modern times also in the interior of the Ferrari program's bestseller. Precious materials dominate the interior; the gears are switched – analogue to Formula 1 – by functional rocker switches on the steering wheel.

meets individual customer wishes with its wide range of interior options, from the colour of the leather to a roll bar or a silver plaque with a personal dedication. There is also inexpensive extravagance to be had for the exterior: how about brake callipers in gold, aluminium grey or even red, so-called "Rosso Corsa"? Then there are also the Scuderia Ferrari emblems countersunk in the front wings, and that for less than an additional 1000 Euros; they should also not be forgotten.

The Modena commends itself as an ideal basis for motor sport. No wonder that a Challenge version for the racetrack soon followed, and later a 360 GTC was homologised for the FIA GT Championship.

Five years after the premiere of the Modena 360 one thing is for sure: thanks to its elegance, paired with an enormous sporting potential and – considering comparable competitors – its favourable price, it is the frontrunner of Ferarri's sales statistics. The statisticians will soon be recording it as the most successful car in the history of the firm.

The twentieth Spider generation of the Ferrari family is exciting in every way, even with a closed top. Whether black, dark blue, grey or beige, the canopy of crease free material has all the sleek appearance of a hardtop. The striptease into an open version lasts a little more than 20 seconds and is stunning, even when repeatedly experienced. On operating a black plastic lever on the middle console a fascinating process of folding and countersinking the canopy is set in motion. After a short to and fro, it disappears into a storage area between the seating and the motor. A gentle "plop" as the tonneau connects to the side humps signals the end of the performance.

The Spider also displays the curvilinear waistline to its best advantage. The fairings imply the start of a roof, which emphasises the waistline. The stable roll bars are embedded in these elevations. As with the Modena, on show under glass: the rev-happy V8 with its 400 bhp. The end of the engine cover with its glass window possesses a flowing edge to achieve almost the same good aerodynamic qualities as the Modena. The engine, very much confined in space by the convertible top's storage area, acquires additional air

Details such as the air intakes at the front and on the sides as well as the diffuser under the characteristic rear testify to the aerodynamic efficiency of the Modena bodywork.

supply through side grills, which in the case of the Spider's motor cover turn out to be especially large. This resolves the thermal sensitivity very well. The intake manifolds with the classical Ferrari covers cuddle up to each other between the air supply conduits in the Spider engine compartment, as opposed to lying apart as with the Modena.

A Spider's statics had already been largely taken into account in the construction of the Modena. The necessary dynamic rigidity is provided by additional side reinforcements and a cross brace in front of the engine. Passenger safety is ensured by a strengthened windscreen frame as well as the roll bars. Thanks to the light aluminium construction throughout, the Spider weighs in with only 60 kg (130 lbs) more than the coupé.

A cabriolet is normally an invitation for Boulevard cruising. But as the Spider's acceleration and top

speeds are quite near the Modena's, there's a great temptation to really give gas. Beyond 150 kph (93 mph) the fresh air experience certainly gives way to "a hurricane dance". The nets which are supposed to protect the head area from swirling back currents lose their effect, and from 200 (124 mph) upwards the passengers' ears flap in the turbulence. The unforgettable sound emanating from the four exhaust pipes mixes with that of the air rushing by to form an incomparable aural backdrop.

The demand was enormous even before delivery began in autumn 2000. For, in the end, the elitist pleasure of being able to tear along – on whatever – at almost 295 kph (183 mph) in an open car is relatively inexpensive when one takes Ferrari's competitors into consideration. Pininfarina's perfect lines are beyond price anyway: timelessly beautiful and yet sportingly aggressive.

The V8 engine with its 3.6-litre capacity and 400 bhp also operates in the Spider. The open 360 offers the possibility to enjoy the fascinating eight-cylinder sound almost unfiltered. Its form is one of unblemished beauty.

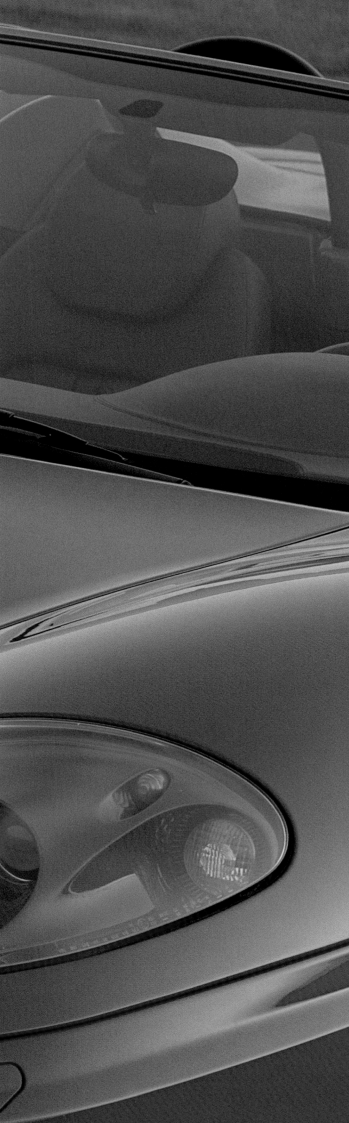

The closed material canopy is worn by the Modena like a small cap, a press on a button suffices to open it, and, after a few seconds, nothing more stands in the way of fresh air pleasure.

Enzo Ferrari

Living next door to one another, they occasionally have a little chat as good neighbours usually do: Giuseppe Petrotta, responsible for limited editions in Ferrari's sacred halls, and Rory Byrne, design engineer in the even more awesome to enter Formula 1 department. Giuseppe and Rory also had to deal with each other officially in the run-up to a new exclusive super sports car, a successor to such famous predecessors as the 288 GTO, F40 and F50. After all, the wealth of experience gathered in Grand-Prix sport should also flow into the project. At first, only the basis of propulsion was definite, a 6 litre V12, and Luca di Montezemolo's ban on spoilers. *Il Presidente* would only tolerate a small retractable contact surface. The stable's best racehorse, Michael Schumacher, completed in the test phase many circuits of Fiorano to ensure that the sports car conceived for a top speed of 350 kph (218 mph) also took the curves as flat as a pancake.

For lack of a company anniversary to mark – as previously with the F40 – the "racer with number plates", limited in number to 399 vehicles, was named after Enzo Ferrari in homage to the company's founder, whose name is immortalised on a small plaque on the edge of the centre console. Sergio Pininfarina set himself a further memorial. He used the minimal scope for creativity left to him by the combined technology and wind tunnel trials in his own

The Enzo Ferrari proudly carries its prominent Formula 1 nose. This vehicle, of which there are only 399 specimens, is the racing car for the road – 355 kph (221 mph) top speed. No one can offer more. The price in summer 2004: 645,000 Euros.

way: inimitably deft, with interesting details and yet aerodynamically efficient from front to rear.

Entering the vehicle through the upwardly swinging vertical doors – as already seen with the 1972 Lamborghini Countach – takes place without causing dislocation. The rider of this steed sinks his behind into an anatomically formed shell which can be ordered in the sizes S, M, L and XL. Everyday car standards such as a remote-controlled central locking system, an electric window lift, a radio or air-conditioning are missing. The interior serves only one purpose: transportation as in a thoroughbred racing car. Focus is concentrated on the steering wheel borrowed from Formula 1, with its flattened upper section in which LEDs begin to dance from 6000 rev upwards, sending a reminder of a change in rhythm. Told off in this manner, the driver is to operate the

It bears a great name, that of the legendary founder of the company, and offers the finest of the fine: carbon body, wheel suspension similar to Formula 1, aerodynamic finesse from sport racing, and naturally a twelve-cylinder engine.

"Up" switch to apply the ultra-fast gear change. The electronic lightshow degrades the rev counter to a mere decoration, and to glance at the speedometer with its red background and scale reaching up to 400 kph (250 mph) is more of an irritation. Travelling at such speed puts you into the red of all road traffic regulations anyway.

All the necessary switches for driving are integrated into the steering wheel: indicator, level control for the front of the vehicle, chassis adjustment, ASR deactivation and even a small button for the reverse gear. The red starter, the trigger of all imaginable and unimaginable speed intoxications high, is enthroned on the upper section of the centre console. It activates the combined force of 660 bhp at 7800 revs. Everything which follows should be transferred to the northern loop of the Nürburgring. Here the Enzo can really feel at home, reaching times of less than eight

minutes, depending on the abilities of the driver. That this vehicle is actually a racing car – as so many Ferraris before it – is shown by its structure: carbon fibre monocoque with aluminium sub frame for the longitudinally mounted 12 cylinders, electro-hydraulic 6-gear transmission, individual wheel suspension with double cross wishbones, pushrod operated struts. Fast speeds demand a corresponding braking ability: brutally displayed by the Formula 1 carbon ceramic brakes, built into a road car for the first time. The consistent air canalisation above, through and under the vehicle – from the pointed nose to the more than two metre- (6½ ft-) wide rear – reflects pure racing car culture. By the way, it was a man from the home of such old Ferrari cavaliers as Gonzalez, Fangio and Reutemann who succeeded in becoming the first Ferrari customer to be allowed to enjoy all this.

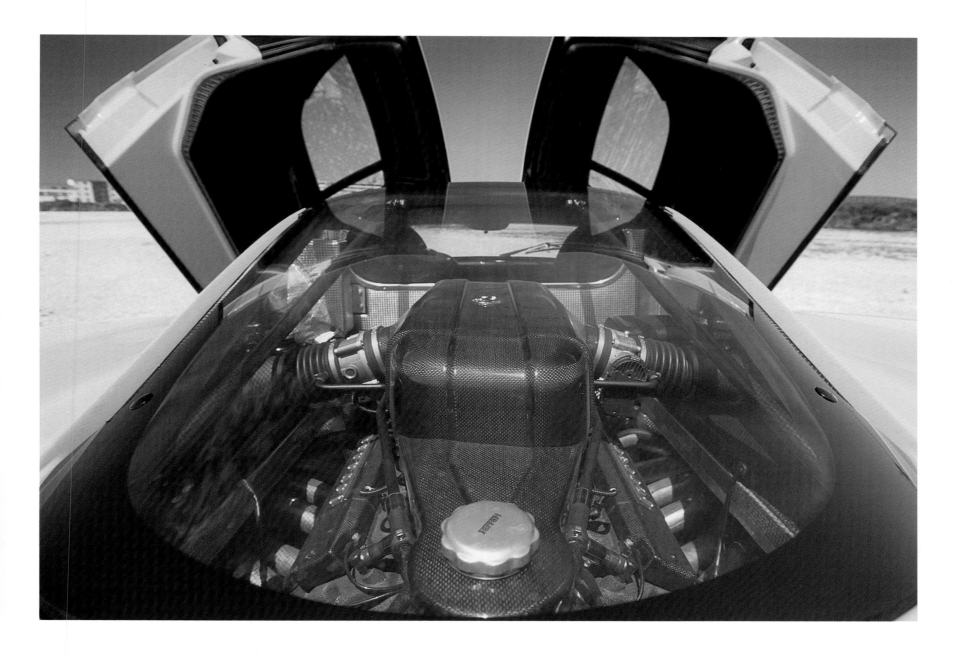

The light doors open upwards and ease entry. Leather and air conditioning convey an air of luxury. Otherwise a functional practicality dominates. One is meant to concentrate on driving.

The extendable rear spoiler and the diffuser behind the sequential six-gear transmission make the aerodynamics visible. The Enzo therewith displays an unshakeable stability, even at over 300 kph (185 mph).

The twelve-cylinder achieves 660 bhp from its six-litre capacity at 7800 rpm. The rear horizontal built-in spring shock absorbers demonstrate pure racing technology. The Enzo catapults itself from 0 to 100 kph (62 mph) in 3.6 seconds.

Challenge Stradale

Since 1993 it has become a custom befitting their standing for well-off gentlemen (occasionally also ladies) with sporting ambitions to pit themselves against each other on the racetrack in equally powerful Ferraris. They can be seen cavorting in the Ferrari-Challenge-Pirelli-Trophy. Following the competition versions of the 348 and F355, they can now own with the 360 Modena Challenge a simply predestined sport machine. That an even more powerful foal has sprung from this racehorse is a reason for joy among the "sporting lads". Normally, racing car derivatives for daily use in traffic turn out to be rather more civil than there racing counterparts. That is not the case with the Challenge Stradale: its engine produces 425 bhp and is therefore the most powerful standard Ferrari V8 of all time. It combines its muscle play with an absolutely infernal background noise. The chassis – 15 millimetres (0.6") lower than that of the 360 Modena – allows lateral acceleration results on a par with a racing car's, and after a sprint to 200 kph (124 mph) in just 15.5 seconds, one can reach the peak: 300 kph (187 mph). Indeed, the greatest challenge with a Challenge Stradale is to behave like a normal road user.

While it was not difficult to save 94 kg (207 lbs) on the aluminium bodywork and interior, slimming down the engine and transmission a further 11 kg (24 lbs) was more difficult. In order to lose 110 kg (243 lbs) in weight, even the unsuspended mass had to shed five kg (11 lbs): in all a cost intensive course of treatment to boost potential, which included the generous use of aluminium as with the roll-bar or the pedals, punch-holed to reduce weight. Titanium

The sports version of the 360 Modena conceals itself behind this term. 25 bhp more powerful, 80 kilograms (175 lbs) lighter, 15 millimetres (0.6") lower, and around 35,000 Euros more expensive. From 0 to 100 is achieved just half a second quicker, and the 300 kph (185 mph) hurdle is taken.

The distinctive optical features of the Challenge Stradale are only the rear carbon shade and the larger wheels. At its fastest, the Formula 1 transmission can change gear in a 150-millisecond step.

springs and wheel bolts and carbo-ceramic punch-holed brake disks: only the best is good enough. The air-conditioning was not on the list of interior amenities to be axed. It is certainly quite useful for keeping a cool head in this "roadrunner".

Sobriety and functionality dominate the cockpit: upholstered carbon fibre racing seats, 4-point racing attachment seat belts with Ferrari emblem, door panels without interior trim, target sight markings on the steering wheel rim, paddle switching, bare sheet metal floors under the thin mats and carbon fibre mounted instruments. Two buttons radiate a magical attraction: the fire red starter and the press button switch with the "race" inscription. Its activation causes gear changing behind the valance at an almost unimaginable speed, somewhere in the range of milli-seconds. The chassis also adjusts itself to racing requirements with the "race on" setting. Nothing against that Formula 1 feeling, but, during a traffic light start with "launch control", that rising lust for *competizione* really should be withstood. Even with the switch in "sport" mode, with its not quite so fast

— but still in millisecond range — gear change and less aggressive damper setting, and aided by traction control (ASR), the Stradale is one big challenge.

The clicking of the paddle switches belongs to the almost inaudible accompanying phenomena of driving. The spellbinding glance at the needle of the rev counter, which can shoot up to the 8500 mark on its bright yellow background, is only seldom interrupted by a short check on acceleration in the carbon fibre housed rear mirror. In dry conditions a borderline tightrope walk is possible with the 7 Zero Corsa

In the silhouette, the expert can identify the side air intakes for engine cooling and induction air as elegant aids for an efficient aerodynamic. Large, perforated ventilated brake disks guarantee optimal braking.

Pirelli sports tyres – narrow on the front and a wide 285/35 on the rear – assuming a high degree of driving ability. Such experiments should definitely not be undertaken in wet conditions, even with traction control. Wet conditions are not the *macchina* from the sunny south's cup of tea.

No limits have been set for the Stradale's production. Its numbers are more than enough to position it in the GT class of international motor sport. In cooperation with Michelotto Automobile, the Ferrari department for racing customers developed the GTC; a wide "winged" racing flatfish, which lies with its 1100 kg (2425 lbs) exactly at the minimum allowed weight. A further 20 bhp has been goaded out of the engine, bringing the total to 445 *cavalli,* which for its competitors is not to be laughed at. This vehicle with its racing tyres and roll cage has no need of a "race" switch – it is built solely for this purpose.

The 425 bhp V8 operates convincingly with an extremely vicious throttle response and a phenomenal torque. Definitely not for the weak of heart. The most important instrument for controlling the V8 is the tachometer with its yellow background.

612 Scaglietti

For him too, a befitting honour: the coachwork artist Sergio Scaglietti, who, in the fifties and sixties of the last century, formed, or rather sculptured, quite a few Ferrari bodies, hammering them into form, chiselling and chipping away, and all done by eye. His most famous piece of work was unique; a 375 MM Berlinetta which was given by director Roberto Rosselini to this lover Ingrid Bergmann as a present. It possessed a similar appearance to the present day 612 Scaglietti which is named after Sergio: a dominant wide lattice mouth, but without the slightly drawn-back lower jaw. A modern coachwork plant has grown up on the outskirts of Modena since the noble sheet metal forge was taken over by Ferrari in 1975. Skilled workmanship is still a guarantee for quality.

The Pininfarina-designed bodywork has to bridge an extraordinary long wheelbase of just about three metres, as the 6 litre V12 has been placed behind the front axle. An additional 252 cc was added by sleight of hand in order to achieve the model identification 612. The transaxle positioning of the engine and transmission, with the passenger cage for four occupants in between, crowns a balanced division of weight, whereby 54 percent rests on the rear axle: ideal for the ESP – or CST *(Controllo Stabilità Trazione)* as it is called by Ferrari – supported cornering. The 612 Scaglietti's curvaceousness has been kept quite within limits. The somewhat plain rear

The tradition of more luxurious, more powerful 2+2 seaters from the noble Maranello manufacturer is carried on without interruption by the incomparable grandezza of the 612 Scaglietti. The most modern bi-xenon lights shine from the covered headlights.

with its traditional pairs of round tail lights hardly raises an eyebrow, which is clearly not the case with the vehicle's front, with ridges running from the plastic casements of the xenon headlights right through to the wings. The scalloped sides, reaching into the door area, are somewhat reminiscent of the latest designs of BMW designer Christopher E. Bangle.

A demure luxury liner with an almost indecent 540 bhp potential is hidden beneath the aluminium body, which has been stretched over an aluminium frame. When this potential is aroused, then it is with such an unobtrusive volume that even the CD player comes into its own. While the available leather seating space at the back is only fitting for small passengers, at the front, even well-built people can enjoy the comfort of this mobile luxury. Five fan jets, set in aluminium, can let loose a virtual hurricane; an equivalent for the hardly noticeable 320 kph (199 mph) on an optimal road surface.

The LCD display penned in on the left of the dashboard does not fit in with the well-proportioned curves of the switches, buttons and tachometer;

although one does wish to know how much Super the *testa rossa* sealed power plant is guzzling. However, if you can afford this 220,000 Euro vehicle, you're hardly likely to suffer a *mal di testa* (headache) when the 20 litre per 100 kilometres (12 mpg) mark is reached. Emergency help of another kind is available from a leather case containing tools and reserve light bulbs situated in the boot, which, with its 240 litre (8½ cu.ft.) volume, provides enough space for two travel bags.

Modern sensors which register rainfall and light and set the necessary reaction in motion, are a prerequisite for comfortable cruising. Driving comfort is also electronically regulated. The F1A automatic gear set up is not everyone's cup of tea. The active-minded may either diligently flip the switches or quite conventionally engage the gears. This long ship can be manoeuvred through narrow stretches quite like a speedboat through the rocks. After all, a Ferrari has to show its colours. However, matching the colour of the brake callipers to that of bodywork is not absolutely necessary.

Indented flanks add suspense to the flowing silhouette of the 612, designed as with all its predecessors by the company designer Pininfarina. With his sure hand he created an elegant Gran Turismo in the great tradition of the brand.

Comfortable seats at the front for relaxed traveling, sufficient room and space at the rear for the children. The magnificent twelve-cylinder with ample capacity (5.75 litres) pampers its passengers with its driving attributes, performance (540 bhp), and temperament in all situations.

Specifications

Spider (Barchetta) Touring
1948–1953: 41 built
212 Export 1951
Chassis number 0084E

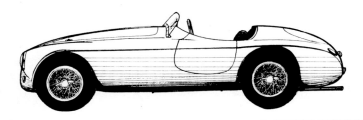

Engine	Configuration	V12 60 degrees, longitudinal front
	Displacement	2562 cc
	Bore and stroke	68 x 58.8 mm
	Fuel system	3 Weber 36 DCF
	Output	170 bhp at 6500 rpm
Gearbox		5-speed, non-synchromesh
Chassis	Frame	welded tubular steel
	Suspension front	independent, unequal-length A-arms, transverse leaf springs
	Suspension rear	live axle, semi-elliptic springs
	Brakes	drums hydraulically operated
Dimensions	Wheelbase	2200 mm
	Length, width, height	4000 x 1600 x 1200 mm
	Weight	900 kg (curb)
Performance	Top speed	approx. 200 kph

Coupé Ghia
1950–1952: 26 built
195 Inter 1950
Chassis number 0105S

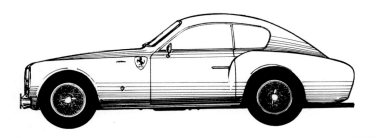

Engine	Configuration	V12 60 degrees, longitudinal front
	Displacement	2341 cc
	Bore and stroke	65 x 58.8 mm
	Fuel system	1 Weber 36 DCF
	Output	135 bhp at 6000 rpm
Gearbox		5-speed, 3rd and 4th synchr.
Chassis	Frame	welded tubular steel
	Suspension front	independent, unequal-length A-arms, leaf springs
	Suspension rear	live axle, semi-elliptic springs
	Brakes	drums hydraulically operated
Dimensions	Wheelbase	2500 mm
	Length, width, height	4100 x 1450 x 1350 mm
	Weight	960 kg (curb)
Performance	Top speed	192 kph
	Acceleration 0–100 kph	9.9 s

Spider Vignale
1951–1953: approx. 60 built
166 MM 1953
Chassis number 0314M

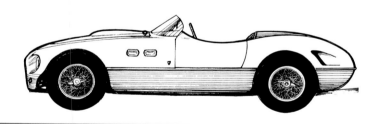

Engine	Configuration	V12 60 degrees, longitudinal front
	Displacement	1995 cc
	Bore and stroke	60 x 58.8 mm
	Fuel system	3 Weber 32 IF4/C
	Output	160 bhp at 7200 rpm
Gearbox		5-speed, non-synchromesh
Chassis	Frame	welded tubular steel
	Suspension front	independent, unequal-length A-arms, transverse leaf springs
	Suspension rear	live axle, semi-elliptic springs
	Brakes	drums hydraulically operated
Dimensions	Wheelbase	2250 mm
	Length, width, height	4100 x 1650 x 1130 mm
	Weight	800 kg (dry)
Performance	Top speed	approx. 200 kph

250 MM Coupé Pinin Farina
1953–1954: 18 built
250 MM Coupé PF 1953
Chassis number 0344MM

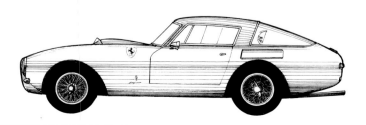

Engine	Configuration	V12 60 degrees, longitudinal front
	Displacement	2953 cc
	Bore and stroke	73 x 58.8 mm
	Fuel system	3 Weber 36 DCF
	Output	240 bhp at 7200 rpm
Gearbox		4-speed, all-synchromesh
Chassis	Frame	welded tubular steel
	Suspension front	independent, unequal-length A-arms, transverse leaf springs
	Suspension rear	live axle, semi-elliptic springs
	Brakes	drums hydraulically operated
Dimensions	Wheelbase	2400 mm
	Length, width, height	3988 x 1600 x 1257 mm
	Weight	945 kg (curb)
Performance	Top speed	208 kph

250 GT Europa Pinin Farina
1953–1956: 41 built
250 GT 1955
Chassis number 0417GT

Engine	Configuration	V12 60 degrees, longitudinal front
	Displacement	2953 cc
	Bore and stroke	73 x 58.8 mm
	Fuel system	3 Weber 36 DC13
	Output	220 bhp at 7000 rpm
Gearbox		4-speed, all-synchromesh
Chassis	Frame	welded tubular steel
	Suspension front	independent, unequal-length A-arms, coil springs
	Suspension rear	live axle, semi-elliptic springs
	Brakes	drums hydraulically operated
Dimensions	Wheelbase	2600 mm
	Length, width, height	4458 x 1676 x 1371 mm
	Weight	1307 kg (with full tank)
Performance	Top speed	205 kph
	Acceleration 0–100 kph	6 s

375 MM Spider, 375 Plus
1953–1954: 15 MM 375 Spider, 6 375 Plus
375 Plus 1954
Chassis number 0396AM

Engine	Configuration	V12 60 degrees, longitudinal front
	Displacement	4954 cc
	Bore and stroke	84 x 74.5 mm
	Fuel system	3 Weber 46 DCF/3
	Output	345 bhp at 6000 rpm
Gearbox		4-speed, all-synchromesh
Chassis	Frame	welded tubular steel
	Suspension front	independent, unequal-length A-arms, transverse leaf springs
	Suspension rear	de Dion axle, transverse leaf springs
	Brakes	drums hydraulically operated
Dimensions	Wheelbase	2600 mm
	Length, width, height	4190 x 1638 x 1092 mm
	Weight	900 kg (dry)
Performance	Top speed	270 kph

750 Monza
1954–1955: 30 built
750 Monza 1954
Chassis number 0462M

Engine	Configuration	4 in line, longitudinal front
	Displacement	2999 cc
	Bore and stroke	103 x 90 mm
	Fuel system	2 Weber 58 DCO A/3
	Output	250 bhp at 6000 rpm
Gearbox		5-speed, non-synchromesh
Chassis	Frame	welded tubular steel
	Suspension front	independent, unequal-length A-arms, transverse leaf springs
	Suspension rear	de Dion axle, transverse leaf springs
	Brakes	drums hydraulically operated
Dimensions	Wheelbase	2250 mm
	Length, width, height	4166 x 1651 x 1054 mm
	Weight	760 kg (dry)
Performance	Top speed	265 kph

410 S Spider and Coupé
1955: 4 built
410 S
Chassis number 0596 CM (Spider), 0595 (Coupé)

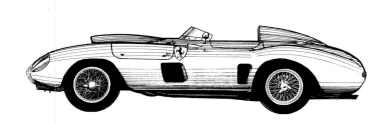

Engine	Configuration	V12 60 degrees, longitudinal front
	Displacement	4961 cc
	Bore and stroke	88 x 68 mm
	Fuel system	3 Weber 46 DCF/3
	Output	380 bhp at 7000 rpm
Gearbox		4-speed, all-synchromesh
Chassis	Frame	welded tubular steel
	Suspension front	independent, unequal-length A-arms, coil springs
	Suspension rear	de Dion axle, transverse leaf springs
	Brakes	drums hydraulically operated
Dimensions	Wheelbase	2350 mm
	Weight	1200 kg (dry)
Performance	Top speed	303.5 kph (1000 km Buenos Aires 1956)

410 Superamerica Series I–III
1956–1959: 37 built
410 SA Series I 1955
Chassis number 0493SA

Engine		in this specimen: 375 MM
	Configuration	V12 60 degrees, longitudinal front
	Displacement	4522 cc
	Bore and stroke	84 x 68 mm
	Fuel system	3 Weber 42 DCZ
	Output	340 bhp at 7000 rpm
Gearbox		4-speed, all-synchromesh
Chassis	Frame	welded tubular steel
	Suspension front	independent, unequal-length A-arms, coil springs
	Suspension rear	live axle, semi-elliptic springs
	Brakes	drums hydraulically operated
Dimensions	Wheelbase	2800 mm
	Weight	1200 kg (dry)
Performance	Top speed	265 kph
	Acceleration 0–100 kph	5.8 s

250 GT Boano/Ellena
1956–1958: 75 Boano, 49 Ellena
250 GT Boano 1957
Chassis number 0675GT

Engine	Configuration	V12 60 degrees, longitudinal front
	Displacement	2953 cc
	Bore and stroke	73 x 58.8 mm
	Fuel system	3 Weber 36 DCZ
	Output	240 bhp at 7000 rpm
Gearbox		4-speed, all-synchromesh
Chassis	Frame	welded tubular steel
	Suspension front	independent, unequal-length A-arms, coil springs
	Suspension rear	live axle, semi-elliptic springs
	Brakes	drums hydraulically operated
Dimensions	Wheelbase	2600 mm
	Length, width, height	4458 x 1676 x 1372 mm
	Weight	1307 kg (with full tank)
Performance	Top speed	203.5 kph
	Acceleration 0–100 kph	6 s

250 GT Tour de France
1956–1959: 84 built
250 GT TdF 1958
Chassis number 1141GT

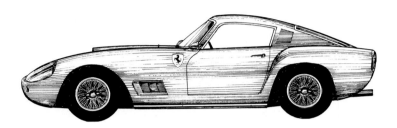

Engine	Configuration	V12 60 degrees, longitudinal front
	Displacement	2953 cc
	Bore and stroke	73 x 58.8 mm
	Fuel system	3 Weber 36 DCZ3
	Output	260 bhp at 7000 rpm
Gearbox		4-speed, all-synchromesh
Chassis	Frame	welded tubular steel
	Suspension front	independent, unequal-length A-arms, coil springs
	Suspension rear	live axle, semi-elliptic springs
	Brakes	drums hydraulically operated
Dimensions	Wheelbase	2600 mm
	Length, width, height	4350 x 1600 x 1350 mm
	Weight	1160 kg (with full tank)
Performance	Top speed	245 kph
	Acceleration 0–100 kph	7.6 s
	Acceleration 0–200 kph	26.3 s

500 Testa Rossa – TRI 62
1956–1962: 70 built
500 TRC 1957
Chassis number 0682TR

Engine	Configuration	4 in line, longitudinal front
	Displacement	1984 cc
	Bore and stroke	90 x 78.8 mm
	Fuel system	2 Weber 40 DCO/A3
	Output	180 bhp at 7000 rpm
Gearbox		4-speed, all-synchromesh
Chassis	Frame	welded tubular steel
	Suspension front	independent, unequal-length A-arms, coil springs
	Suspension rear	live axle, coil springs
	Brakes	drums hydraulically operated
Dimensions	Wheelbase	2250 mm
	Length, width, height	3937 x 1638 x 965 mm
	Weight	680 kg (dry)
Performance	Top speed	approx. 245 kph

290 S, 315 S, 335 S
1957: 7 built
335 S 1957
Chassis number 0674

Engine	Configuration	V12 60 degrees, 4 overhead camshafts, longitudinal front
	Displacement	4023 cc
	Bore and stroke	77 x 72 mm
	Fuel system	6 Solex 40 PII
	Output	390 bhp at 7800 rpm
Gearbox		4-speed, all-synchromesh
Chassis	Frame	welded tubular steel
	Suspension front	independent, unequal-length A-arms, coil springs
	Suspension rear	de Dion axle, transverse leaf springs
	Brakes	drums hydraulically operated
Dimensions	Wheelbase	2350 mm
	Length, width, height	4204 x 1651 x 1041 mm
	Weight	880 kg (dry)
Performance	Top speed	approx. 300 kph

250 GT Cabriolet Series I and II
1957–1962: 242 built
250 GT Cabriolet Series II 1961
Chassis number 2489GT

Engine	Configuration	V12 60 degrees, longitudinal front
	Displacement	2953 cc
	Bore and stroke	78 x 58.8 mm
	Fuel system	3 Weber 36 DCL
	Output	240 bhp at 7000 rpm
Gearbox		4-speed, all-synchromesh with electrically operated overdrive (5th)
Chassis	Frame	welded tubular steel
	Suspension front	independent, unequal-length A-arms, coil springs
	Suspension rear	live axle, semi-elliptic springs
	Brakes	discs
Dimensions	Wheelbase	2600 mm
	Length, width, height	4700 x 1690 x 1330 mm
	Weight	1200 kg (dry)
Performance	Top speed	225 kph

250 GT California Spyder Series I and II
1957–1962: 108 built
250 GT California Spyder SWB 1961
Chassis number 2537GT

Engine	Configuration	V12 60 degrees, longitudinal front
	Displacement	2953 cc
	Bore and stroke	73 x 58.8 mm
	Fuel system	3 Weber 40 DCL/6
	Output	280 bhp at 7000 rpm
Gearbox		4-speed, all-synchromesh
Chassis	Frame	welded tubular steel
	Suspension front	independent, unequal-length A-arms, coil springs
	Suspension rear	live axle, semi-elliptic springs
	Brakes	discs
Dimensions	Wheelbase	2400 mm
	Length, width, height	4200 x 1720 x 1370 mm
	Weight	1050 kg (dry)
Performance	Top speed	248 kph

250 GT Coupé Pinin Farina
1958–1960: 343 built
250 GT Coupé PF 1958
Chassis number 1083GT

Engine	Configuration	V12 60 degrees, longitudinal front
	Displacement	2953 cc
	Bore and stroke	73 x 58.8 mm
	Fuel system	3 Weber 36 DCL
	Output	240 bhp at 7000 rpm
Gearbox		4-speed, all-synchromesh
Chassis	Frame	welded tubular steel
	Suspension front	independent, unequal-length A-arms, coil springs
	Suspension rear	live axle, semi-elliptic springs
	Brakes	drums hydraulically operated
Dimensions	Wheelbase	2600 mm
	Length, width, height	4700 x 1725 x 1340 mm
	Weight	1150 kg (dry)
Performance	Top speed	201.6 kph
	Acceleration 0–100 kph	6 s

250 GT Berlinetta SWB
1959–1962: 167 built
250 GT Berlinetta SWB 1961
Chassis number 3129GT

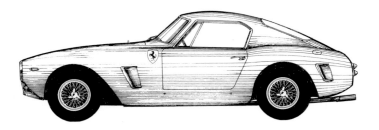

Engine	Configuration	V12 60 degrees, longitudinal front
	Displacement	2953 cc
	Bore and stroke	73 x 58.8 mm
	Fuel system	3 Weber 36 DCL
	Output	280 bhp at 7000 rpm
Gearbox		4-speed, all-synchromesh
Chassis	Frame	welded tubular steel
	Suspension front	independent, unequal-length A-arms, coil springs
	Suspension rear	live axle, semi-elliptic springs
	Brakes	discs
Dimensions	Wheelbase	2400 mm
	Length, width, height	4150 x 1690 x 1260 mm
	Weight	1120 kg (with full tank)
Performance	Top speed	233 kph
	Acceleration 0–100 kph	8.2 s
	Acceleration 0–200 kph	24.3 s

400 Superamerica
1959–1963: 45 built
400 SA Coupé Aerodinamico 1962
Chassis number 2861SA

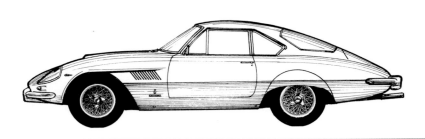

Engine	Configuration	V12 60 degrees, longitudinal front
	Displacement	3967 cc
	Bore and stroke	77 x 71 mm
	Fuel system	3 Weber 40 DCL/6
	Output	340 bhp at 7000 rpm
Gearbox		4-speed, all-synchromesh with electrically operated overdrive (5th)
Chassis	Frame	welded tubular steel
	Suspension front	independent, unequal-length A-arms, coil springs
	Suspension rear	live axle, semi-elliptic springs
	Brakes	discs
Dimensions	Wheelbase	2600 mm
	Length, width, height	4670 x 1770 x 1300 mm
	Weight	1362 kg (with full tank)
Performance	Top speed	272 kph
	Acceleration 0–100 kph	9.4 s

250 GTE Coupé 2+2
1960–1963: 955 built (+ 49 330 America)
250 GTE Coupé 2+2 1962
Chassis number 3989GT

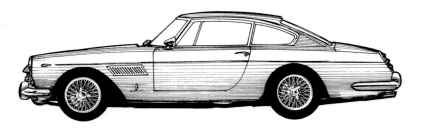

Engine	Configuration	V12 60 degrees, longitudinal front
	Displacement	2953 cc
	Bore and stroke	73 x 58.8 mm
	Fuel system	3 Weber 36 DCS
	Output	240 bhp at 7000 rpm
Gearbox		4-speed, all-synchromesh with electrically operated overdrive (5th) only with axle ratio 4.57
Chassis	Frame	welded tubular steel
	Suspension front	independent, unequal-length A-arms, coil springs
	Suspension rear	live axle, semi-elliptic springs
	Brakes	discs
Dimensions	Wheelbase	2600 mm
	Length, width, height	4700 x 1700 x 1350 mm
	Weight	1488 kg (with full tank)
Performance	Top speed	219.5 kph
	Acceleration 0–100 kph	8.5 s
	Acceleration 0–200 kph	37 s

Dino 246 SP, 196 SP, 286 SP, 248 SP, 268 SP

1961–1962: 7 built
Dino 268 SP 1962
Chassis number 0798

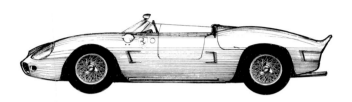

Engine	Configuration	V8 90 degrees, longitudinal rear
	Displacement	2645 cc
	Bore and stroke	77 x 71 mm
	Fuel system	4 Weber 40 IF2/C
	Output	260 bhp at 7500 rpm
Gearbox		5-speed, non-synchromesh
Chassis	Frame	welded tubular steel
	Suspension front	independent, unequal-length A-arms, coil springs
	Suspension rear	independent, unequal-length A-arms, coil springs
	Brakes	discs
Dimensions	Wheelbase	2320 mm
	Length, width, height	3828 x 1582 x 1022 mm
	Weight	870 kg (dry)
Performance	Top speed	290 kph

250 GTO Series I and II

1962–1964: 36 Series I, 3 Series II
250 GTO Series I 1963
Chassis number 4153

Engine	Configuration	V12 60 degrees, longitudinal front
	Displacement	2953 cc
	Bore and stroke	73 x 58.8 mm
	Fuel system	6 Weber 38 DCN
	Output	297 bhp at 7400 rpm
Gearbox		5-speed, 2nd–5th synchromesh
Chassis	Frame	welded tubular steel
	Suspension front	independent, unequal-length A-arms, coil springs
	Suspension rear	live axle, semi-elliptic springs
	Brakes	discs
Dimensions	Wheelbase	2400 mm
	Length, width, height	4325 x 1600 x 1210 mm
	Weight	900 kg (dry)
Performance	Top speed	250 kph
	Acceleration 0–100 kph	5.6 s
	Acceleration 0–200 kph	20.1 s

250 GT Lusso

1962–1964: 354 built
250 GT Lusso 1963
Chassis number 5147GT

Engine	Configuration	V12 60 degrees, longitudinal front
	Displacement	2953 cc
	Bore and stroke	73 x 58.8 mm
	Fuel system	3 Weber 36 DCS
	Output	250 bhp at 7000 rpm
Gearbox		4-speed, all-synchromesh
Chassis	Frame	welded tubular steel
	Suspension front	independent, unequal-length A-arms, coil springs
	Suspension rear	live axle, semi-elliptic springs
	Brakes	discs
Dimensions	Wheelbase	2400 mm
	Length, width, height	4410 x 1750 x 1290 mm
	Weight	1363 kg (with full tank)
Performance	Top speed	240 kph
	Acceleration 0–100 kph	8.2 s

250 LM
1963–1965: 32 built
250 LM 1964
Chassis number 5841

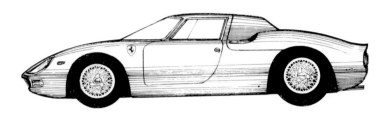

Engine	Configuration	V12 60 degrees, longitudinal rear
	Displacement	3286 cc
	Bore and stroke	77 x 58.8 mm
	Fuel system	6 Weber 38 DCN
	Output	320 bhp at 7700 rpm
Gearbox		5-speed, non-synchromesh
Chassis	Frame	welded tubular steel
	Suspension front	independent, unequal-length A-arms, coil springs
	Suspension rear	independent, unequal-length A-arms, coil springs
	Brakes	discs
Dimensions	Wheelbase	2400 mm
	Length, width, height	4270 x 1700 x 1115 mm
	Weight	820 kg (dry)
Performance	Top speed	287 kph (axle ratio: 3.548 : 1)

330 GT 2+2
1964–1967: 1057 built
330 GT 2+2 1964
Chassis number 5561GT

Engine	Configuration	V12 60 degrees, longitudinal front
	Displacement	3967 cc
	Bore and stroke	77 x 71 mm
	Fuel system	3 Weber 40 DFI
	Output	300 bhp at 6600 rpm
Gearbox		4-speed, all-synchromesh, with electrically operated overdrive (5th)
Chassis	Frame	welded tubular steel
	Suspension front	independent, unequal-length A-arms, coil springs
	Suspension rear	live axle, coil and semi-elliptic springs
	Brakes	discs
Dimensions	Wheelbase	2650 mm
	Length, width, height	4840 x 1715 x 1365 mm
	Weight	1380 kg (curb)
Performance	Top speed	234 kph
	Acceleration 0–100 kph	6.9 s
	Acceleration 0–200 kph	29 s

500 Superfast
1964–1966: 37 built
500 Superfast 1964
Chassis number 6049

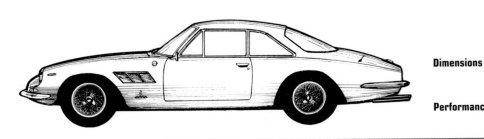

Engine	Configuration	V12 60 degrees, longitudinal front
	Displacement	4962 cc
	Bore and stroke	88 x 68 mm
	Fuel system	3 Weber 40 DCZ/6
	Output	400 bhp at 6500 rpm
Gearbox		5-speed, all-synchromesh
Chassis	Frame	welded tubular steel
	Suspension front	independent, unequal-length A-arms, coil springs
	Suspension rear	live axle, coil and semi-elliptic springs
	Brakes	discs
Dimensions	Wheelbase	2650 mm
	Length, width, height	4820 x 1780 x 1280 mm
	Weight	1400 kg (curb)
Performance	Top speed	280 kph
	Acceleration 0–100 kph	8 s

275 GTB, 275 GTS, 275 GTB/4, Spider NART
1964–1968: 1007 built
275 GTB/4 1967
Chassis number 10855

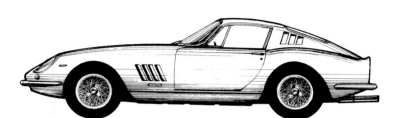

Engine	Configuration	V12 60 degrees, 4 overhead camshafts, longitudinal front
	Displacement	3286 cc
	Bore and stroke	77 x 58.8 mm
	Fuel system	6 Weber 40 DCN
	Output	300 bhp at 8000 rpm
Gearbox		5-speed, all-synchromesh
Chassis	Frame	welded tubular steel
	Suspension front	independent, unequal-length A-arms, coil springs
	Suspension rear	independent, unequal-length A-arms, coil springs
	Brakes	discs
Dimensions	Wheelbase	2400 mm
	Length, width, height	4410 x 1725 x 1200 mm
	Weight	1050 kg (curb)
Performance	Top speed	260 kph
	Acceleration 0–100 kph	5.6 s

275/330 P, 275/330 P2, 330 P3, 330 P4
1965–1967: 12 built
330 P4 1967
Chassis number 0860

Annotation: This car was modified to participate in CanAm racing with Chris Amon driving and then restored to P4 configuration in 1970.

Engine	Configuration	V12 60 degrees, 4 overhead camshafts, 3 valves per cylinder, longitudinal rear
	Displacement	3967 cc
	Bore and stroke	77 x 71 mm
	Fuel system	injection
	Output	450 bhp at 8200 rpm
Gearbox		5-speed, all-synchromesh
Chassis	Frame	welded tubular steel reinforced with alloy panels
	Suspension front	independent, unequal-length A-arms, coil springs
	Suspension rear	independent, unequal-length A-arms, coil springs
	Brakes	ventilated discs
Dimensions	Wheelbase	2400 mm
	Length, width, height	4185 x 1810 x 1000 mm
	Weight	800 kg (dry)
Performance	Top speed	320 kph

330 GTC, 330 GTS, 365 GTC, 365 GTS
1966–1970: 874 built
365 GTC 1969
Chassis number 12571

Engine	Configuration	V12 60 degrees, longitudinal front
	Displacement	4390 cc
	Bore and stroke	81 x 71 mm
	Fuel system	3 Weber 40 DFI
	Output	320 bhp at 6600 rpm
Gearbox		5-speed, all-synchromesh
Chassis	Frame	welded tubular steel
	Suspension front	independent, unequal-length A-arms, coil springs
	Suspension rear	independent, unequal-length A-arms, coil springs
	Brakes	discs
Dimensions	Wheelbase	2400 mm
	Length, width, height	4470 x 1670 x 1300 mm
	Weight	1300 kg (curb)
Performance	Top speed	243 kph
	Acceleration 0–100 kph	6.4 s

365 California
1966–1967: 14 built
365 California 1966
Chassis number 8347

Engine	Configuration	V12 60 degrees, longitudinal front
	Displacement	4390 cc
	Bore and stroke	81 x 71 mm
	Fuel system	3 Weber 40 DFI
	Output	320 bhp at 6600 rpm
Gearbox		5-speed, all-synchromesh
Chassis	Frame	welded tubular steel
	Suspension front	independent, unequal-length A-arms, coil springs
	Suspension rear	live axle, coil and semi-elliptic springs
	Brakes	discs
Dimensions	Wheelbase	2650 mm
	Length, width, height	4900 x 1780 x 1330 mm
	Weight	1320 kg (curb)
Performance	Top speed	245 kph

Dino 206 S
1966: 16 built
Dino 206 S 1966
Chassis number 010

Engine	Configuration	V6 65 degrees, 4 overhead camshafts, longitudinal rear
	Displacement	1987 cc
	Bore and stroke	86 x 57 mm
	Fuel system	injection
	Output	220 bhp at 9000 rpm
Gearbox		5-speed, non-synchromesh
Chassis	Frame	welded tubular steel, reinforced
	Suspension front	independent, unequal-length A-arms, coil springs
	Suspension rear	independent, unequal-length A-arms, coil springs
	Brakes	discs
Dimensions	Wheelbase	2280 mm
	Length, width, height	3875 x 1680 x 985 mm
	Weight	580 kg (dry)
Performance	Top speed	260 kph

350 CanAm, 612 CanAm, 712 CanAm
1967–1971: 2 P4 modified, 1 512 M modified
712 CanAm 1971
Chassis number 1010

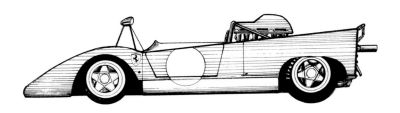

Engine	Configuration	V12 60 degrees, 4 overhead camshafts, 4 valves per cylinder, longitudinal rear
	Displacement	6900 cc
	Fuel system	injection
	Output	720 bhp at 8000 rpm
Gearbox		5-speed, all-synchromesh
Chassis	Frame	semi-monocoque with alloy panels
	Suspension front	independent, unequal-length A-arms, single lower arms, radius rods, coil springs
	Suspension rear	independent, single upper and lower arms, radius rods, coil springs
	Brakes	ventilated discs
Dimensions	Wheelbase	2400 mm
	Length, width, height	4360 x 2190 x 970 mm
	Weight	680 kg (dry)
Performance	Top speed	340 kph

365 GT 2+2
1967–1971: 800 built
365 GT 2+2 1968
Chassis number 11213

Engine	Configuration	V12 60 degrees, longitudinal front
	Displacement	4390 cc
	Bore and stroke	81 x 71 mm
	Fuel system	3 Weber 40 DFI
	Output	320 bhp at 6600 rpm
Gearbox		5-speed, all-synchromesh
Chassis	Frame	welded tubular steel reinforced with sheet metal
	Suspension front	independent, unequal-length A-arms, coil springs
	Suspension rear	independent, unequal-length A-arms, coil springs, hydro-pneumatic levelling device
	Brakes	discs
Dimensions	Wheelbase	2650 mm
	Length, width, height	4980 x 1790 x 1345 mm
	Weight	1825 kg (with full tank)
Performance	Top speed	244 kph
	Acceleration 0–100 kph	7.3 s

Dino 206 GT, 246 GT, 246 GTS
1967–1974: 3913 built
Dino 246 GT 1972
Chassis number 03288

Engine	Configuration	V6 65 degrees, 4 overhead camshafts, transversal rear
	Displacement	2418 cc
	Bore and stroke	92.5 x 60 mm
	Fuel system	3 Weber 40 DCF 14
	Output	195 bhp at 7500 rpm
Gearbox		5-speed
Chassis	Frame	welded tubular steel
	Suspension front	independent, unequal-length A-arms, coil springs
	Suspension rear	independent, unequal-length A-arms, coil springs
	Brakes	ventilated discs
Dimensions	Wheelbase	2340 mm
	Length, width, height	4230 x 1700 x 1115 mm
	Weight	1230 kg (with full tank)
Performance	Top speed	238.4 kph
	Acceleration 0–100 kph	7.4 s

365 GTB/4 Daytona, GTS/4 Daytona
1968–1973: 1395 built
365 GTS/4 Daytona 1971
Chassis number 16475

Engine	Configuration	V12 60 degrees, 4 overhead camshafts, longitudinal front
	Displacement	4390 cc
	Bore and stroke	81 x 71 mm
	Fuel system	6 Weber 40 DCN 20
	Output	348 bhp at 7500 rpm
Gearbox		5-speed
Chassis	Frame	welded tubular steel
	Suspension front	independent, unequal-length A-arms, coil springs
	Suspension rear	independent, unequal-length A-arms, coil springs
	Brakes	discs
Dimensions	Wheelbase	2400 mm
	Length, width, height	4425 x 1760 x 1245 mm
	Weight	1625 kg (with full tank)
Performance	Top speed	274.8 kph
	Acceleration 0–100 kph	6.1 s
	Acceleration 0–200 kph	21.8 s

312 P
1968–1969: 2 built
312 P 1969
Chassis number 0870

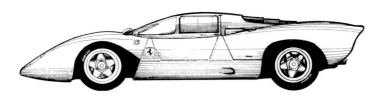

Engine	Configuration	V12 60 degrees, 4 overhead camshafts, 4 valves per cylinder, longitudinal rear
	Displacement	2989 cc
	Bore and stroke	77 x 53.5 mm
	Fuel system	injection
	Output	430 bhp at 9800 rpm
Gearbox		5-speed, all-synchromesh
Chassis	Frame	semi-monocoque
	Suspension front	independent, unequal-length A-arms, coil springs
	Suspension rear	independent, unequal-length A-arms, coil springs
	Brakes	ventilated discs
Dimensions	Wheelbase	2370 mm
	Length, width, height	4230 x 1980 x 950 mm
	Weight	680 kg (dry)
Performance	Top speed	320 kph

512 S, 512 M
1969–1970: 25 built
512 M 1970
Chassis number 1018

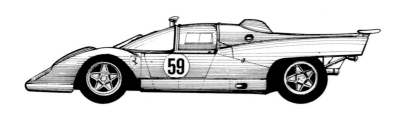

Engine	Configuration	V12 60 degrees, 4 overhead camshafts, 4 valves per cylinder, longitudinal rear
	Displacement	4994 cc
	Bore and stroke	87 x 70 mm
	Fuel system	injection
	Output	610 bhp at 9000 rpm
Gearbox		5-speed
Chassis	Frame	semi-monocoque
	Suspension front	independent, unequal-length A-arms, coil springs
	Suspension rear	independent, unequal-length A-arms, coil springs
	Brakes	ventilated discs
Dimensions	Wheelbase	2400 mm
	Length, width, height	4360 x 2000 x 970 mm
	Weight	930 kg (curb)
Performance	Top speed	340 kph

312 PB
1970–1973: 12 built
312 PB 1972
Chassis number 0884

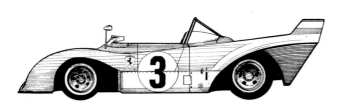

Engine	Configuration	flat 12, 4 overhead camshafts, 4 valves per cylinder, longitudinal rear
	Displacement	2991 cc
	Bore and stroke	80 x 49.6 mm
	Fuel system	injection
	Output	440 bhp at 11000 rpm
Gearbox		5-speed
Chassis	Frame	semi-monocoque
	Suspension front	independent, upper A-arms, wide-base lower A-arms, coil springs
	Suspension rear	independent, single upper links, lower A-arms, long parallel radius rods, coil springs
	Brakes	ventilated discs
Dimensions	Wheelbase	2220 mm
	Length, width, height	3770 x 1960 x 954 mm
	Weight	655 kg (dry)
Performance	Top speed	320 kph

365 GTC/4
1971–1972: 493 built
365 GTC/4 1971
Chassis number 15547

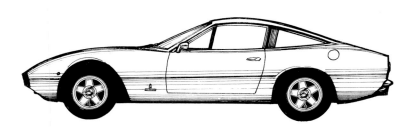

Engine	Configuration	V12 60 degrees, 4 overhead camshafts, longitudinal front
	Displacement	4390 cc
	Bore and stroke	81 x 71 mm
	Fuel system	6 Weber 38 DCOE
	Output	320 bhp at 6200 rpm
Gearbox		5-speed
Chassis	Frame	welded tubular steel
	Suspension front	independent, unequal-length A-arms, coil springs
	Suspension rear	independent, unequal-length A-arms, coil springs
	Brakes	discs
Dimensions	Wheelbase	2550 mm
	Length, width, height	4570 x 1780 x 1270 mm
	Weight	1877 kg (with full tank)
Performance	Top speed	244 kph
	Acceleration 0–100 kph	7.5 s

365 GT4 BB, BB 512, BB 512i
1971–1984: 2323 built
BB 512i 1984
Chassis number 50667

Engine	Configuration	flat 12, 4 overhead camshafts, longitudinal rear
	Displacement	4943 cc
	Bore and stroke	82 x 78 mm
	Fuel system	injection
	Output	340 bhp at 6000 rpm
Gearbox		5-speed
Chassis	Frame	welded tubular steel
	Suspension front	independent, unequal-length A-arms, coil springs
	Suspension rear	independent, unequal-length A-arms, coil springs
	Brakes	ventilated discs
Dimensions	Wheelbase	2500 mm
	Length, width, height	4400 x 1830 x 1120 mm
	Weight	1600 kg (with full tank)
Performance	Top speed	288 kph
	Acceleration 0–100 kph	5.9 s
	Acceleration 0–200 kph	20.7 s

365 GT4 2+2, 400i, 412
1972–1989: 2911 built
412 1986
Chassis number 65855

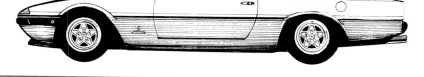

Engine	Configuration	V12 60 degrees, 4 overhead camshafts, longitudinal front
	Displacement	4943 cc
	Bore and stroke	82 x 78 mm
	Fuel system	injection
	Output	340 bhp at 6000 rpm
Gearbox		5-speed
Chassis	Frame	welded tubular steel
	Suspension front	independent, unequal-length A-arms, coil springs
	Suspension rear	independent, unequal-length A-arms, coil springs
	Brakes	ventilated discs
Dimensions	Wheelbase	2700 mm
	Length, width, height	4810 x 1800 x 1315 mm
	Weight	1805 kg (curb)
Performance	Top speed	250 kph
	Acceleration 0–100 kph	6.7 s
	Acceleration 0–200 kph	26.7 s

Dino 308 GT4
1973–1980: 3656 built
Dino 308 GT4 1976
Chassis number 13676

Engine	Configuration	V8 90 degrees, 4 overhead camshafts, transversal rear
	Displacement	2927 cc
	Bore and stroke	81 x 71 mm
	Fuel system	4 Weber 40 DCNF
	Output	236 bhp at 7700 rpm
Gearbox		5-speed
Chassis	Frame	welded tubular steel
	Suspension front	independent, unequal-length A-arms, coil springs
	Suspension rear	independent, unequal-length A-arms, coil springs
	Brakes	ventilated discs
Dimensions	Wheelbase	2550 mm
	Length, width, height	4320 x 1800 x 1180 mm
	Weight	1320 kg (with full tank)
Performance	Top speed	248.3 kph
	Acceleration 0–100 kph	6.8 s
	Acceleration 0–200 kph	28.5 s

308 GTB, 308 GTS, 328 GTB, 328 GTS
1975–1989: 21,678 built
308 GTB 1979
Chassis number 26983

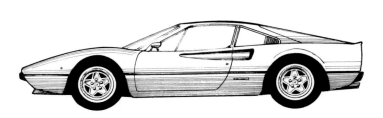

Engine	Configuration	V8 90 degrees, 4 overhead camshafts, transversal rear
	Displacement	2927 cc
	Bore and stroke	81 x 71 mm
	Fuel system	4 Weber 40 DCNF
	Output	255 bhp at 7700 rpm
Gearbox		5-speed
Chassis	Frame	welded tubular steel
	Suspension front	independent, unequal-length A-arms, coil springs
	Suspension rear	independent, unequal-length A-arms, coil springs
	Brakes	ventilated discs
Dimensions	Wheelbase	2340 mm
	Length, width, height	4230 x 1720 x 1120 mm
	Weight	1320 kg (with full tank)
Performance	Top speed	255.3 kph
	Acceleration 0–100 kph	6.5 s
	Acceleration 0–200 kph	25.9 s

Mondial 8, 3.2, t, Cabriolet
1980–1993: 6156 built
Mondial 3.2 1989
Chassis number 76286

Engine	Configuration	V8 90 degrees, 4 overhead camshafts, 4 valves per cylinder, transversal rear
	Displacement	3185 cc
	Bore and stroke	83 x 73.6 mm
	Fuel system	injection
	Output	270 bhp at 7000 rpm
Gearbox		5-speed
Chassis	Frame	welded tubular steel
	Suspension front	independent, unequal-length A-arms, coil springs
	Suspension rear	independent, unequal-length A-arms, coil springs
	Brakes	ventilated discs
Dimensions	Wheelbase	2650 mm
	Length, width, height	4535 x 1795 x 1235 mm
	Weight	1410 kg (curb)
Performance	Top speed	254 kph
	Acceleration 0–100 kph	6.7 s
	Acceleration 0–200 kph	28.4 s

288 GTO
1984–1986: 272 built
288 GTO 1985
Chassis number 53317

Engine	Configuration	V8 90 degrees, 4 overhead camshafts, 4 valves per cylinder, 2 turbochargers with intercoolers, longitudinal rear
	Displacement	2855 cc
	Bore and stroke	80 x 71 mm
	Fuel system	injection
	Output	400 bhp at 7000 rpm
Gearbox		5-speed
Chassis	Frame	welded tubular steel
	Suspension front	independent, unequal-length A-arms, coil springs
	Suspension rear	independent, unequal-length A-arms, coil springs
	Brakes	ventilated discs
Dimensions	Wheelbase	2450 mm
	Length, width, height	4290 x 1910 x 1120 mm
	Weight	1317 kg (curb)
Performance	Top speed	303 kph
	Acceleration 0–100 kph	4.8 s
	Acceleration 0–200 kph	16.2 s

Testarossa, 512 TR, F512 M
1984–1996: 9937 built (Testarossa and TR)
F512 M 1995
Chassis number 101461

Engine	Configuration	flat 12, 4 overhead camshafts, 4 valves per cylinder, longitudinal rear
	Displacement	4942 cc
	Bore and stroke	82 x 78 mm
	Fuel system	injection
	Output	440 bhp at 6750 rpm
Gearbox		5-speed
Chassis	Frame	welded tubular steel
	Suspension front	independent, unequal-length A-arms, coil springs
	Suspension rear	independent, unequal-length A-arms, coil springs
	Brakes	ventilated discs
Dimensions	Wheelbase	2550 mm
	Length, width, height	4480 x 1975 x 1135 mm
	Weight	1631 kg (curb)
Performance	Top speed	305 kph
	Acceleration 0–100 kph	5.1 s
	Acceleration 0–200 kph	15.7 s

F40
1987–1992: 1311 built
F40 1990
Chassis number 83272

Engine	Configuration	V8 90 degrees, 4 overhead camshafts, 4 valves per cylinder, 2 turbochargers with intercoolers, longitudinal rear
	Displacement	2936 cc
	Bore and stroke	82 x 69.5 mm
	Fuel system	injection
	Output	478 bhp at 7000 rpm
Gearbox		5-speed
Chassis	Frame	steel alloy tubes integrated with sections in composite materials
	Suspension front/rear	independent, unequal-length A-arms, coil springs
	Brakes	ventilated discs
Dimensions	Wheelbase	2450 mm
	Length, width, height	4430 x 1980 x 1130 mm
	Weight	1254 kg (curb)
Performance	Top speed	321 kph
	Acceleration 0–100 kph	4.6 s
	Acceleration 0–200 kph	11 s

348 GTB, 348 GTS, Speciale, 348 Spider
1989–1994: 9485 built
348 ts 1992
Chassis number 93322

Engine	Configuration	V8 90 degrees, 4 overhead camshafts, 4 valves per cylinder, longitudinal rear
	Displacement	3405 cc
	Bore and stroke	85 x 75 mm
	Fuel system	injection
	Output	300 bhp at 7000 rpm
Gearbox		5-speed
Chassis	Frame	monocoque, rear tubular subframe
	Suspension front	independent, unequal-length A-arms, with control arms and coil springs
	Suspension rear	independent, unequal-length A-arms, with control arms and coil springs
	Brakes	ventilated discs
Dimensions	Wheelbase	2450 mm
	Length, width, height	4230 x 1895 x 1170 mm
	Weight	1420 kg (curb)
Performance	Top speed	277 kph
	Acceleration 0–100 kph	5.6 s
	Acceleration 0–200 kph	19.9 s

456 GT, 456M GT, 456M GTA
1992–2002: 3287 built
456 GT 1994
Chassis number 99394

Engine	Configuration	V12 65 degrees, 4 overhead camshafts, 4 valves per cylinder, longitudinal front
	Displacement	5474 cc
	Bore and stroke	88 x 75 mm
	Fuel system	injection
	Output	442 bhp at 6250 rpm
Gearbox		6-speed
Chassis	Frame	welded tubular steel in unit with aluminium body
	Suspension front	independent, unequal-length A-arms, coil springs
	Suspension rear	independent, unequal-length A-arms, double coil spring/damper units
	Brakes	ventilated discs
Dimensions	Wheelbase	2600 mm
	Length, width, height	4730 x 1920 x 1300 mm
	Weight	1790 kg (curb)
Performance	Top speed	302 kph
	Acceleration 0–100 kph	5.2 s
	Acceleration 0–200 kph	18.2 s

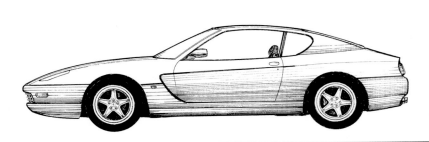

F333 SP
1994–1995: 12 built
F333 SP 1995
Chassis number 012

Engine	Configuration	V12 65 degrees, 4 overhead camshafts, 5 valves per cylinder, longitudinal rear
	Displacement	3997 cc
	Bore and stroke	85 x 58.7 mm
	Fuel system	injection
	Output	over 650 bhp at 11000 rpm
Gearbox		5-speed, sequential mechanical gearshift
Chassis	Frame	stress-bearing chassis in carbon fibre composite and aluminium honeycomb
	Suspension front/rear	independent pushrod-rocker suspension
	Brakes	ventilated discs
Dimensions	Wheelbase	2740 mm
	Length, width, height	4775 x 1994 x 1016 mm
	Weight	860 kg (curb)
Performance	Top speed	298 kph
	Acceleration 0–100 kph	3.7 s
	Acceleration 0–200 kph	10.5 s

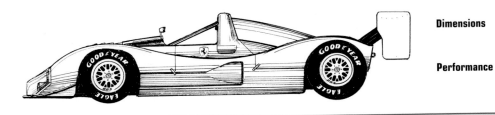

F355 Berlinetta/GTS/Spider/Challenge
1994–1998: 11,258 built
F355 Spider 1995
Chassis number 102080

Engine	Configuration	V8 90 degrees, 4 overhead camshafts, 5 valves per cylinder, longitudinal rear
	Displacement	3496 cc
	Bore and stroke	85 x 77 mm
	Fuel system	injection
	Output	380 bhp at 8200 rpm
Gearbox		6-speed
Chassis	Frame	monocoque, rear tubular subframe
	Suspension front	independent, unequal-length A-arms, coil springs
	Suspension rear	independent, unequal-length A-arms, coil springs
	Brakes	ventilated discs
Dimensions	Wheelbase	2450 mm
	Length, width, height	4250 x 1900 x 1170 mm
	Weight	1512 kg (curb)
Performance	Top speed	295 kph
	Acceleration 0–100 kph	5.3 s
	Acceleration 0–200 kph	18 s

F50
1995–1997: 349 built
F50 1995
Chassis number 99999

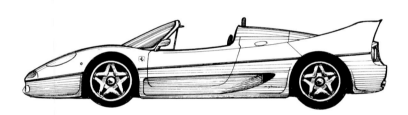

Engine	Configuration	V12 65 degrees, 4 overhead camshafts, 5 valves per cylinder, longitudinal rear
	Displacement	4698 cc
	Bore and stroke	85 x 69 mm
	Fuel system	injection
	Output	520 bhp at 8500 rpm
Gearbox		6-speed
Chassis	Frame	composite material with carbon fibre, Kevlar and Nomex honeycomb, rear tubular subframe
	Suspension front/rear	independent, A-arms and reaction arms that act on spring and damper by way of a push-rod system
	Brakes	ventilated discs
Dimensions	Wheelbase	2580 mm
	Length, width, height	4480 x 1986 x 1120 mm
	Weight	1230 kg (curb)
Performance	Top speed	325 kph
	Acceleration 0–100 kph	3.87 s

550, 575M
from 1996
575M Maranello 2002
Chassis number 128286

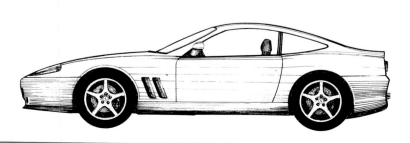

Engine	Configuration	V12 65 degrees, 4 overhead camshafts, 4 valves per cylinder, longitudinal front
	Displacement	5748 cc
	Bore and stroke	89 x 77 mm
	Fuel system	injection
	Output	515 bhp at 7215 rpm
Gearbox		6-speed, F1 electro-hydraulic automatic
Chassis	Frame	welded tubular steel in unit with aluminium body
	Suspension front/rear	independent, double triangular arms, coaxial coil springs with electronic control units
	Brakes	ventilated discs
Dimensions	Wheelbase	2500 mm
	Length, width, height	4550 x 1935 x 1277 mm
	Weight	1730 kg (curb)
Performance	Top speed	325 kph
	Acceleration 0–100 kph	4.25 s

550

2001–2002: 448 built
550 Barchetta Pininfarina 2001
Chassis number 124259

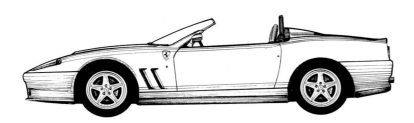

Engine	Configuration	V12 65 degrees, 4 overhead camshafts, 4 valves per cylinder, longitudinal front
	Displacement	5474 cc
	Bore and stroke	86 x 79 mm
	Fuel system	injection
	Output	485 bhp at 7000 rpm
Gearbox		6-speed
Chassis	Frame	welded tubular steel in unit with aluminium body
	Suspension front/rear	independent, double triangular arms, coaxial coil springs with electronic control units
	Brakes	ventilated discs
Dimensions	Wheelbase	2500 mm
	Length, width, height	4550 x 1935 x 1258 mm
	Weight	1690 kg (curb)
Performance	Top speed	300 kph
	Acceleration 0–100 kph	4.4 s

360

from 1999
360 Modena 2000
Chassis number 120900

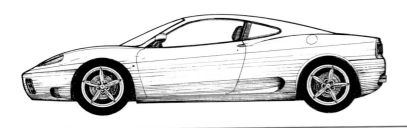

Engine	Configuration	V8 90 degrees, 4 overhead camshafts, 5 valves per cylinder, longitudinal rear
	Displacement	3586 cc
	Bore and stroke	85 x 79 mm
	Fuel system	injection
	Output	400 bhp at 8500 rpm
Gearbox		6-speed manual or F1 electro-hydraulic automatic
Chassis	Frame	aluminium space frame, engine subframe
	Suspension front/rear	independent, adjustable suspension with dual aluminium wishbones, aluminium dampers with an electronic unit control
	Brakes	ventilated discs
Dimensions	Wheelbase	2600 mm
	Length, width, height	4477 x 1992 x 1214 mm
	Weight	1390 kg (curb)
Performance	Top speed	299 kph
	Acceleration 0–100 kph	4.5 s

360

from 2000
360 Spider 2003
Chassis number 132870

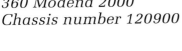

Engine	Configuration	V8 90 degrees, 4 overhead camshafts, 5 valves per cylinder, longitudinal rear
	Displacement	3586 cc
	Bore and stroke	85 x 79 mm
	Fuel system	injection
	Output	400 bhp at 8500 rpm
Gearbox		6-speed or F1 electro-hydraulic automatic
Chassis	Frame	aluminium space frame, engine subframe
	Suspension front/rear	independent, adjustable suspension with dual aluminium wishbones, aluminium dampers with an electronic unit control
	Brakes	ventilated discs
Dimensions	Wheelbase	2600 mm
	Length, width, height	4477 x 1992 x 1235 mm
	Weight	1450 kg
Performance	Top speed	295 kph
	Acceleration 0–100 kph	4.6 s

Enzo Ferrari
from 2002: 399 built
Enzo Ferrari 2002
Chassis number 132649

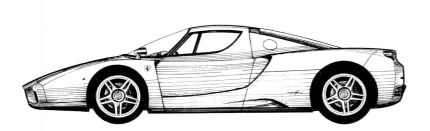

Engine	Configuration	V12 65 degrees, 4 overhead camshafts, 4 valves per cylinder, longitudinal rear
	Displacement	5998 cc
	Bore and stroke	92 x 75.2 mm
	Fuel system	injection
	Output	660 bhp at 7800 rpm
Gearbox		6-speed, F1 electro-hydraulic automatic
Chassis	Frame	carbon fibre monocoque, rear tubular subframe
	Suspension front/rear	independent, double triangular arms that act on springs and by way of a push-rod system
	Brakes	ventilated carbon ceramics discs
Dimensions	Wheelbase	2650 mm
	Length, width, height	4702 x 2035 x 1147 mm
	Weight	1365 kg (curb)
Performance	Top speed	350 kph
	Acceleration 0–100 kph	3.65 s

360
from 2003
Challenge Stradale 2003
Chassis number 134349

Engine	Configuration	V8 90 degrees, 4 overhead camshafts, 5 valves per cylinder, longitudinal rear
	Displacement	3586 cc
	Bore and stroke	85 x 79 mm
	Fuel system	injection
	Output	425 bhp at 8500 rpm
Gearbox		6-speed, F1 electro-hydraulic automatic
Chassis	Frame	aluminium space frame, engine subframe
	Suspension front/rear	independent, adjustable suspension with dual aluminium wishbones, aluminium dampers with an electronic unit control
	Brakes	ventilated discs
Dimensions	Wheelbase	2600 mm
	Length, width, height	4477 x 1922 x 1199 mm
	Weight	1280 kg
Performance	Top speed	over 300 kph
	Acceleration 0–100 kph	4.1 s

612 Scaglietti
from 2004
612 Scaglietti 2004
Chassis number 136337

Engine	Configuration	V12 65 degrees, 4 overhead camshafts, 4 valves per cylinder, longitudinal behind front axle
	Displacement	5748 cc
	Bore and stroke	89 x 77 mm
	Fuel system	injection
	Output	540 bhp at 7250 rpm
Gearbox		6-speed, manual or F1-A electro-hydraulic automatic
Chassis	Frame	aluminium space frame
	Suspension front/rear	independent, double triangular arms, dampers with coaxial coil springs, CST electronic stability and traction control system
	Brakes	ventilated discs
Dimensions	Wheelbase	2950 mm
	Length, width, height	4902 x 1957 x 1344 mm
	Weight	1840 kg
Performance	Top speed	320 kph
	Acceleration 0–100 kph	4.2 s

For their unflagging support and enthusiasm we would like to thank
Dr. Darius Ahrabian · Jean-Jacques Bailly · Pierre Bardinon · Mario Bernardi
Andreas Birner · Henri Chambon · Adriano Cimarosti · David Cottingham
Diethelm Doll · Jürgen Dorschner · Helmut Eberlein · Herbert Engel · Jochen Frick
Michael Gabel · Ennio Gianaroli Peter Gläsel · Hubert Hahne · Maria Homann
Lukas Hüni · Hartmut Ibing · Manfred Jung · Peter Kaus · Reinhard Kehm
Thomas Kellermann · Roland Kessler · Thomas Kiesele · Stephan Köhler
Uwe Meissner · Gerd Meranius · Hans Mischler · Karl Müller · Martha Naudascher
Albert Obrist · Holger Richter · Jean Sage · Walter Schäfer · Klaus Scholtyssek
Ulf Schossow · Jürgen Schultzke · Christoph, Engelbert & Heinz Stieger
Klaus Ulrich · Hans-Jürgen Zapf

Photographs: Rainer W. Schlegelmilch
Text: Hartmut Lehbrink, Schalkenbach
      Jochen von Osterroth, Oberwesel (p. 10–19, p. 328–399)
Translation: Russell Cennydd
Layout and typography: Oliver Hessmann
Cover: Oliver Hessmann
Project management: Joachim Schwochert
Drawings: Jochen von Osterroth
Historical photographs: Archiv Diethelm Doll (p. 10–18)
Photographs p.19: Ferrari Deutschland, Wiesbaden

*KÖNEMANN is a registered trademark of Tandem Verlag GmbH

Printed in Germany
ISBN 3-8331-1231-x (original German edition)
ISBN 3-8331-1057-0 (English edition)

10 9 8 7 6 5 4 3 2
X IX VIII VII VI V IV III II I